GOOD JEWISH GIRL:

A JERUSALEM LOVE STORY GONE BAD

GOOD JEWISH GIRL:
A JERUSALEM LOVE STORY GONE BAD

Liz Rose Shulman

with a foreword by Ilan Pappe

Querencia Press — Chicago IL

QUERENCIA PRESS

© Copyright 2025
Liz Rose Shulman

All Rights Reserved

No reproduction, copy or transmission of this publication may be made without written permission.
No paragraph of this publication may be reproduced, copied, or transmitted save with the written permission of the author.

Any person who commits any unauthorized act in relation to this publication may be liable to criminal prosecution and civil claims for damages.

ISBN 978 1 963943 32 0

www.querenciapress.com

First Published in 2025

Querencia Press, LLC
Chicago IL

Printed & Bound in the United States of America

Praise for *Good Jewish Girl: A Jerusalem Love Story Gone Bad*

Liz Rose Shulman's book delves into the intricate journey of distinguishing Zionism from Judaism through a social justice lens. Through sincere discussions of love, family, and cultural displacement, this book offers her moving personal experience of disagreement, compassion, and the challenges of the Israeli-Palestinian conflict.

—Manal Yazbak Abu Ahmad, Ph.D.

A "good Jewish girl" is one who loyally supports the exclusionary, Zionist project in Palestine. Shulman's book challenges this racist notion and argues for an inclusive future out of this racist frame that has characterized the settler-colonial project between the Jordan River and the Mediterranean since its establishment.

—Haidar Eid, Alaqsa University, Gaza, Palestine

Liz Rose Shulman is part of a new generation of American Jews who have been painfully renegotiating their relationship to Zionism and the State of Israel. In these moving, intimate and gorgeously written essays, Shulman charts her own personal renegotiation of this issue, illuminating how the political can be so deeply, achingly intertwined with the personal.

—Brant Rosen

Liz Rose Shulman's book tells a story that many American Jews will recognize—being educated in Jewish schools and Jewish summer camps to adore Israel and forget Palestine. She makes leaps in time and space to tell a story that is still unfolding. Her transformation occurs, in many ways, through her body, where the sexualization of Israel is a strategic part of the Israel-project that American Jews are subjected to. Liz offers us an honest journey with the whole of her being—body, mind, and soul—a journey that is required of those who seek to escape their Zionist indoctrination.

—Jonathan Ofir

Good Jewish Girl provides invaluable insights into the process of indoctrination into a nationalist ideology through religion, sexuality and much more. With skillful storytelling, poetic turns of phrase and a rich knowledge of the subject matter, Liz Shulman informs and engages.

—Rabbi Michael Davis

Liz Shulman isn't the first author to narrate her breakup with Israel. But she does so with humor, decency and painful honesty—a spirit that will move readers of all ideological stripes.

—Peter Beinart, author, *Being Jewish After the Destruction of Gaza*

Refreshingly raw and captivating in its storytelling, Liz Shulman's intimate self-portrait offers a powerful account of identity made through relationships—not just with people, but with a place (Jerusalem) and an idea (Zionism). Unafraid to be authentic in her erotic entanglements and honest in her journey, Shulman's account humanizes the complexity of identity politics as she traverses the contentious terrain of one of the world's most enduring conflicts. In a voice that is accessible, inviting, and unassumingly wise, Shulman's collection of essays brilliantly invites empathy, frustration, despair—and still somehow a sense of hope in its radical honesty.

—Phillip L. Hammack, author of *Narrative and the Politics of Identity: The Cultural Psychology of Israeli and Palestinian Youth* and Professor of Psychology, University of California, Santa Cruz

Good Jewish Girl: A Jerusalem Love Story Gone Bad is a significant voice in contemporary Jewish literature. Shulman's seemingly innocent love for Israel becomes romantic when as a teen she visits and later attends grad school in Jerusalem. In a conversational, sometimes lyrical—always honest and thoughtful—voice, Shulman writes of her friendships, love affairs, and the myths and truths she learns as she begins to question what she has been taught. By the end, Shulman thinks differently about Zionism, but her strong Jewish identity remains intact. A greatly compelling read, replete with wry humor and wise insights.

—Garnett Kilberg-Cohen

For a just peace in Israel and Palestine and everywhere

For my parents, and for Tony

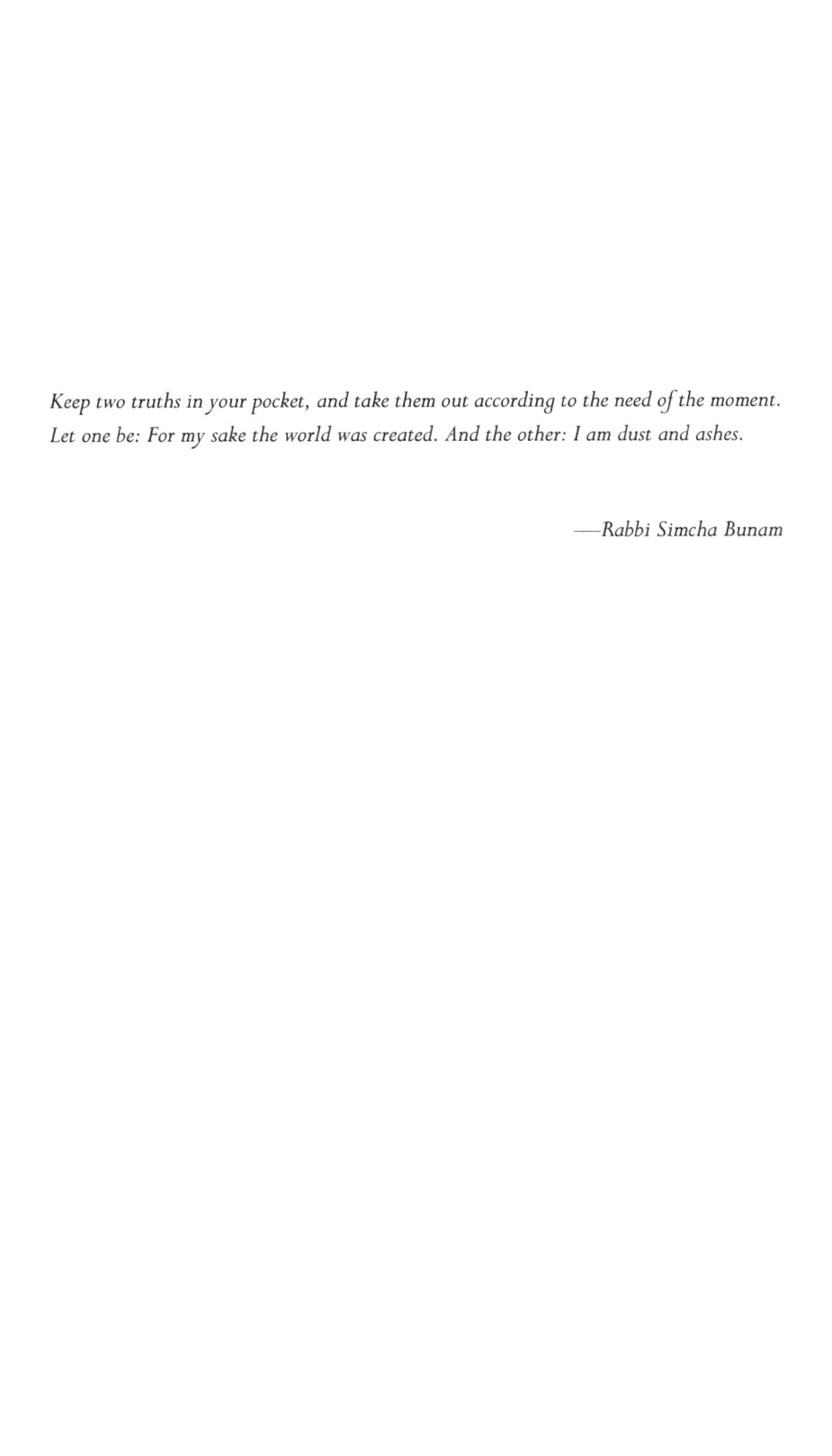

Keep two truths in your pocket, and take them out according to the need of the moment. Let one be: For my sake the world was created. And the other: I am dust and ashes.

—*Rabbi Simcha Bunam*

April, 1994

Dear Lizzy,

I can't begin to tell you how much I am looking forward to seeing you in Jerusalem. And I will wait for June because the timing will be good for both of us, the weather will be perfect for sipping tea outside, the Jerusalem gold will be clearer and last longer than it will in January. I love you, Lizzy. You'll write, not just papers for your classes, but your stories and letters and journal entries for future stories.

Love,

Mom

September, 1994

Dear Mom,

I hope that at some point when I get home that we can sit down and I can talk to you about my experiences. I think it is important to see and bear witness, and I need to find a way to continue who I have become here, *how* I have become here. I've always been interested in the other side, but Jerusalem has changed me. You are so rational and logical and I know you think I only came here to get a degree. I'll have it. I will, but it really is so much more than that.

Love,

Liz

CONTENTS

Foreword 14
Preface 17

Good Jewish Girl 23
A Jerusalem Love Story Gone Bad: Searching for Cigarettes in Jerusalem .. 34
Bravado on a Hill 44
The Stamp Collector 48
While He Was Stopped by Soldiers: Another Jerusalem Love Story Gone Bad 57
Was Dracula Jewish? 66
A Meandering, Sometimes Agonizing Path 78
16-Year Old Love Story: Once I Was Lit by Moonbeams 91
Holy Land Harps 99
"Rose-Red City Half as Old as Time" 108
It's Their Birthright 121
"I didn't think of the pink light or the stones at dusk" 128
Early Love Story: How Many More Orgasms Will be Had for Zionism? . 137
O Jerusalem, Please Forget Me 145
Good Jewish Boys and Girls: My First Porno 151
My Russia Ukraine 162
The Nazis Are Coming 172

Acknowledgments 183
Notes on Previous Publications 184
Thanks 185

Foreword

A journey out of one's tribal boundaries as well as outside one's comfort zone is never an easy trajectory. This book tells the story of such a journey which will be familiar for Jews and Israelis who incrementally found themselves in direct clash with Zionism in all its manifestations.

I walked on a similar path myself and can recognize Liz's moments of bewilderment, embarrassment, anxiety on the one hand, and a growing sense of doing the right thing, and being confident that there is no way back, on the other.

There is no moment of epiphany. Looking back at being an Israeli Jew or an American Jew who spent long spells in Israel, it is not all bleak and negative. There are friends from the past, there are moments of joy, but all in all, this is a mature review of living in a comfort zone with an apartheid state that committed daily crimes against the Palestinians from its very moment of inception in 1948.

There are many ways in which one can describe these journeys. In her outstanding book, *Beyond Tribal Boundaries*, Abigail Abarbanel shared with us twenty-five such stories, including one by myself, each told a different story on the way out of Zionism into either a world of Judaism as a universal worldview or into the sphere of activism on behalf of the Palestinians.

What is unique about Liz's compassionate, humorous, and moving account is that it is more open about how humanity defeats ideological barriers, such as the one posed by strict ideologies such as Zionism. Romantic encounters and intimate friendships carve a unique path, very humane and funny at times, out of the Zionist comfort zone. The challenges are huge, but it is the mixture of a certain moral constitution and the willingness to learn and unlearn that makes sure the journey does not end until it is completed. This individual story and similar ones are relevant for understanding the bigger picture, in particular when thinking about American Jews and their relationship with Zionism.

There are several discrete processes that are occurring in Israel and Palestine that were accelerated by the events of October 7, 2023. These processes have the potential to change the reality on the ground in a fundamental way.

These processes include the growing international isolation of Israel, the social dissolution of the Israeli Jewish society from within, the weakness of the economy, and the inability of the army to properly defend the state and its citizens. One of the additional important and discrete processes is the change of the attitude of Jews around the world, and in particular young American Jews, towards Israel and Zionism.

The trend to jettison previous loyalties and adherence to Zionism is likely to grow exponentially, given the way the neo-Zionist messianism is taking over Israel, and with it, the wish to be part of a historical corrective, namely joining the solidarity movement with the Palestinians.

Redefining Judaism without Zionism has been for a while an intellectual and scholastic exercise, but it is slowly becoming a moral and political position that will not only define Judaism in the future, but also the Jewish collective in Israel and Palestine.

So, you can enjoy the book as a very intriguing experience of a young person mainly during the 1990s, the period her views have transformed because of the very accessible and riveting style, but you can also ponder beyond the individual story and try and see the bigger picture.

New realities are not only made by great ideas and powerful social movements, it is also the individual journeys as the one so vividly and humanely described here by Liz that would be part of something much larger than just a change in one individual's life. Because it is so authentic, and would resonate with normal and natural life—no revolutionary histrionics and dramatic heroism—it is a powerful example of a road many more will take in the future.

—Ilan Pappe

PREFACE

I began working on this book several years prior to October 7, 2023. Though that day was shocking, it was not surprising. Left-wing groups in Israel and Palestine had been warning for years about Gaza, about how unsustainable it was to keep Palestinians behind a fence in an open-air prison—a much more extreme version of the fences, and later, walls, running through Palestinian villages and towns throughout the West Bank. The ongoing genocide is not surprising either. The conflict continues to be the result of the imbalanced collision of two groups having both experienced existential insecurities for decades—one with great military power and one without.

In March, 2024, I went to Israel and Palestine to spend time with the Israeli, Palestinian, and Armenian friends I met thirty years ago—some of whom are in this book—and to hear their stories of how they are navigating the war. Since my return to the U.S., I've been asking myself what it looks like to be an American Jew who has separated from Zionism. This question is a particularly potent one after October 7.

Unfortunately, I don't like what I see. Zionism and Judaism are being conflated within the Zionist Jewish community, and the same conflation is occurring among many on the left. We must continue to make the distinction between Zionism and Judaism. They are not synonymous. One of the consequences of this conflation is that Jews all over the world are being held responsible for what Israel is doing. The reality is that many Jews around the world do not support the occupation or the war on Gaza. Most of us want a ceasefire, the hostages returned, and a right of return for both Palestinians and Israelis with full and equal rights. Holding Jews responsible for what Israel is doing leads us to the anti-Semitism we've already been witnessing.

The word anti-Zionism is also used throughout this book—another word that has been used and misused since October 7. Words themselves have range, and we risk being reductive if we don't allow for true nuance. Anti-Zionism is not anti-Semitism, yet these also have lacked nuance in the current discourse in the U.S. I hope the nuances of how I use the word throughout the book are clear. Most of all, I defer defining such terms to the people actually living in Israel/Palestine—the people for whom the conflict is hitting the hardest.

True solidarity demands we continue to carry our respective, and different, burdens. For me, this means continuing to understand how I learned and then unlearned Zionism, and what this signifies for me now, as a Jew in the U.S. It means knowing that it is impossible to understand Gaza without understanding Israel and the Nakba. It means listening. It means understanding that everyone has their own grief.

It was 1986. I was 16, and on my first trip to Jerusalem. I stood in front of Apple Pizza on Luntz Street near Ben Yehuda's pedestrian mall, swaying to Naomi Shemer's 1967 song, "Jerusalem of Gold" ("Yerushalayim Shel Zahav") with other young teens in Jerusalem on an eight-week high school program. The song was being played on a boombox and I sang along with other American Jews who had, like me, fallen in love with the city. Rather than hold a lighter up to the music, we held each other's waists and gave a little extra squeeze for those we had crushes on. We were in love with Jerusalem and with each other, too, as our hips moved to the music, our feet firmly planted on the limestone street.

Shemer's famous ballad, commissioned by the mayor of Jerusalem at the time, Teddy Kollek, was first performed at an Israeli Song Festival the night after Israel's independence day on May 15, 1967, just three weeks before Israel's Six-Day War. After the war, Shemer added a final verse about capturing the city, and the song became a nationalistic war-cry of the Israel Defense Forces—a celebration of Jerusalem's reunification—when Israel took the Old City and East Jerusalem.

In many ways, the whole notion of Israel is a nationalistic war-cry—its ongoing occupation, settler-expansion, colonization, and ethnic cleansing of Palestine. As the scholar Ilan Pappe writes in *The Ethnic Cleansing of Palestine* (2006), Israel's goal since the 1882 First Zionist Congress was, and still is, to have as much of Palestine as possible with as few Palestinians as possible. The Israeli government still goes to great, and exorbitantly expensive lengths to get young Jews to love Israel—especially young Jews in the United States. No one questioned Israel's policies towards Palestinians when I was on the eight-week summer program in 1986. We talked about Israel as a miracle that had defied the odds against it. Mostly, we talked about love. In a postcard I sent to my parents in Chicago, that summer in 1986, I wrote about Jerusalem's beauty. It was like nowhere I'd ever seen. "Postcards just don't do this city justice," I wrote. "The golden hue everywhere makes me feel that I've come home."

The essays in this collection are my attempt to understand how the larger historical and political context of Israel and Palestine has shaped, and divided, my life. I was taught at an early age to think critically, to question the status quo, and to challenge others when I felt an injustice. Yet I was, at the same time, also trained to block out possible dissent. I knew—intuitively, perhaps, without language—never to ask about Israel's motives. When I did start to question, and subsequently began to publish essays about my changing relationship with Israel, I received death threats at my workplace from a man in the Jewish community who lived near where I grew up. Like many other Jews who have taken a stand on Palestine, I was also called anti-Semitic, self-hating, and a traitor. Similarly devastating was the fear of a rupture between my parents and me. When I became critical of Israel, I worried that my parents, the very people who taught me to think critically, would never forgive me. I feared it was as though I had turned on them like a zombie eating its own flesh—the very flesh that had created me.

Zionism's heartstrings had a strong pull. On the same summer trip in 1986, several of us sang Shemer's song spontaneously on top of Masada after hiking up the mountain at sunrise, a rite of passage for young Zionists who visit Israel. We chanted the lyrics, "If I forget thee / golden city / Jerusalem of gold..." while the sun cast gold, pink, and orange streaks across the horizon. The sky looked like Homer's dawn in *The Odyssey* spreading "her rose-red fingers." A few of us ran off as others carried the tune, and we made out, pressing ourselves against the stone ruins. In between our kisses, leaning on the ancient rock, we whispered, "If I forget thee...," unclear at the time if these words were meant for each other, or for our beloved golden Jerusalem. Even when we were 90 minutes away in the desert, we felt a love for Jerusalem like the kind Joan Didion feels for New York City in her famous essay, "Goodbye

To All That." "I mean I was in love with the city," she confesses, "the way you love the first person who touches you and never love anyone quite that way again." I can't remember the name of the guy I made out with on top of Masada, but I have etched into my memory every nook and crevice of Jerusalem that I stepped on and played in when I was 16.

This was Zionism's plan, of course, to get young Zionists like me to fall in love unconditionally with the tiny country. Their efforts succeeded; we fell in line like good soldiers. We were expected to grow up and donate money, plant trees—which I did as a child, with my allowance money—buy homes, visit often, perhaps lose our virginity in the holy land (if we hadn't already at the Zionist-Socialist camp we attended in the U.S.) and later, marry a Jew, have kids, maybe make aliyah, and hope for the same things for our Jewish children.

Loving Israel was effortless, uncomplicated, unconditional, different from loving any other country in the world. My non-Jewish friends who professed their love for America, for example, loved it in a way that was different from my romance with Israel. They teased that I talked about Israel like it was my lover. I scoffed at them though they were right. Another postcard I sent to my parents in 1986 did sound as though Jerusalem and I were in love. "Jerusalem and I are getting along just fine!" I wrote, as though we were a married couple who'd been together for decades. It was so much more than simply loving one's country, and you could only understand if you, too, were both Zionist and Jewish.

Besides, we'd developed a way of being together, with private jokes and experiences from our trip. We remembered Elan, the hot soldier many of us wanted to make out with who only made out with Jackie, who annoyed us because she was so pretty. Or Shlomo, the bald tour guide who protected us on the bus with his M16, and the funny way he'd get mad trying to get us to shut up, his M16 rattling against his thigh, as he told us Israel's one-sided history from the comfort of our air-conditioned bus. None of us disputed anything we learned on that trip. We were in an infatuated fugue state with the nation-state, and were surrounded by people who felt the same.

Many of the stories in this collection are about separating from community and family—the price of dissenting. They are also about separating

Zionism from Judaism, a severance that divided my sense of self in half. The book confronts misunderstandings of place and misinterpretations of history, who has access and who is denied, indigeneity and colonialism. Above all, Zionism has been a catastrophe for Palestinians. It has resulted in generational trauma, expulsion, and displacement. Zionism has been harmful to Jews in a very different way. "No one colonizes innocently," Aimé Césaire wrote in his 1955 *Discourse on Colonialism*. Zionism hurts people, and it hurts varyingly.

Even though I am no longer a Zionist, it has left its mark on me like an old blueprint. The deep neural pathways in my brain are still wired, it seems, to remember what it felt like to be Zionist because it was my default frame of reference when I was young. I can't shake it, but I don't think I'm supposed to. Many of us use our former selves to understand who we've grown into. The process is never linear, is always more complex than it seems. Though I have often felt this to be a burden, I have come to think of it as an asset because it helps me understand others—especially those in the community I am from, the community I am no longer a part of, who have a hard time criticizing Israel. Dialogue is vital if there is to be true peace for Palestine, and I take the responsibility seriously. Some of these essays were written when I was younger and more cynical about whether or not people can change. I have shifted my position on this. Young Jewish people tell me all the time they don't have the "Zionist baggage" of the older generation. They are engaged in more dialogue about settler-colonialism and systemic racism. They have preceded me by decades, and will have to fight for justice longer.

Finally, these essays are about love. Love for family, for place and for the people you were told not to fall in love with but who you fell in love with anyway. The kind of love you'll imagine writing about someday because you need badly to understand it in its entirety. Because you need to understand why the greatest love stories are the most painful love stories. You need to understand why they go so badly, why you have to let them go.

GOOD JEWISH GIRL

If I had known that inviting a Palestinian man from East Jerusalem into my parents' hotel room in West Jerusalem minutes after they'd left would make me a bad Jewish girl, I might not have done it. Or maybe I'd have done it. I'm not really sure. What I do know was that I wasn't thinking about all that. My parents had been visiting me from Chicago for 10 days and then they were gone and I felt a bit lost. We all do dumb things when we are lonely, and I really liked Salim. The dumb thing wasn't that I was a Jewish girl who was hanging out with a Palestinian guy. I didn't yet know my personal decisions would also be political ones. The dumb thing was that I invited Salim to the same hotel room my parents had just left. I had always been a good Jewish girl, or so I thought, and while asking Salim to join me made me a bad Jewish girl, I think the truth was that I was just a curious and sad Jewish girl. My parents had left at 1:00 am for the airport, so the room was already paid for. Checkout time was 11:00 am. Salim came right over and we slept in the sheets where my parents had just slept.

This was 1994, and I had been living in Jerusalem for a couple of years. Ten days before Salim joined me in the hotel room, I took the hour-long bus ride, the 485, and greeted my parents with yellow flowers at Ben Gurion airport, at the double doors where the tourists exit. The flowers I got for them that morning still smelled sweet. The next day, with the humidity, they would be pungent. I wore the wide purple and green paisley cotton pants I bought for five dollars in the Arab market a year before. "I bargained the guy down from ten dollars," I bragged to my parents in the sherut, or shared taxi, once I'd done the shekel-to-dollar conversion in my head. The sherut took us from the airport to the hotel I had booked for them in Jerusalem. I made the comment about bargaining in the Arab market (it's called the shuk, I told them) because I wanted to appear to my parents like a local instead of a tourist. At the time of my parents' visit, I had known Salim a couple of months and was only beginning to understand the stories of the Palestinian shop owners who worked in the shuk. I would change a lot after my parents' visit and even more during the years I lived in Jerusalem. As a result, my relationship with my parents would suffer in profound ways as I began to question the whole notion of what it means to be a good Jewish girl.

Growing up a good Jewish girl meant that I loved Israel and was an ardent Zionist. I believed in Israel as a Jewish homeland. Israel had been a desert, I was told by my family, teachers at Hebrew school, counselors at camp, elders at the synagogue. No one had lived there, they told me. The tiny country was a light unto the nations, they said. It can never do any wrong, they insisted. When I was a child, I stared at the map of Israel on my bedroom wall and it soothed me like a baby mobile above a crib. I dreamed of visiting and saved my allowance money to plant trees to help the forests there grow. I worked summer jobs to help pay for my first trip at age 16. I was in love with this faraway land and longed from afar like an unrequited lover. Judaism and Zionism were synonymous to me. Who could blame our parents for wanting us to have successful Jewish lives? Ultimately, they just wanted to know that we'd be self-sufficient, that we'd be okay, that we'd be good Jews.

My parents and I took the shared sherut and not the bus. Determined to show them that I'd been mindful with money while living abroad, my compromise between an expensive taxi and the bus was the shared car service. I knew about the sherut service, I told them with bravado, because I'd been living there already a couple of years. Our seats bounced from the weak shock absorbers as we made our way up towards Jerusalem. As we drove the hills became taller and it felt as though we became smaller. Another couple fussed with their baby, who was starting to cry. As we ascended into the hills, the driver turned off the air conditioning, opened the windows so the car could better handle the ascent, and shifted gears.

"I bargained in Hebrew," I said proudly, smiling and leaning towards my parents as though giving them some sort of intel, "for the pants." I sported a confidence that indicated, at least in my own mind, with no doubt whatsoever, that I was no longer a tourist in Israel. I knew where the locals were. Recently, an Israeli had stopped me on the street and asked me for the time in Hebrew. My friends and I joked that this was the ultimate non-touristy compliment.

I'd spoken Hebrew with the shop owner who sold me the pants because at the time I didn't understand that he was Palestinian and that he spoke Arabic, and that the only reason he talked with me in Hebrew was because it was how he made a living. At the time, the Arab shop owners in the market were—to American Jewish girls like me—background, like unused old props no longer needed for a current show. We had arrived believing we knew the land, for we had loved it from afar our whole lives.

"It's what you do here," I said to my parents in the sherut about my bargaining with the Arab shop owner, schooling them, possibly for the first time in my life, on the ins and outs of being a local. "You're supposed to argue with them," I said. "Like a game." In a few more months, when my disenchantment with Zionism had progressed further, I'd be horrified by these remarks I had made, that I'd reduced a man's ability to make a living in a system where his family had been living under a military occupation for decades to a game. My parents must have cringed for different reasons when I told them about the game. They were undoubtedly exhausted—the direct flight from Chicago to Tel-Aviv takes about eleven hours—and certainly didn't need me to inform them on the ins and outs of travel as soon as they arrived. Besides, it was they who had taught me to travel, had instilled in me a desire to learn about new places and to expand my sense of the world, so my need to instruct them while we were in the sherut was more about my own insecurity rather than their ignorance. Yet in this moment I did know more than them. My mother clutched her handbag and looked curiously out the window at this new terrain she'd only seen photos of her whole life. My good friend Danny, who would meet my parents in a few days for dinner, would later tell me that my father, no matter what he was doing, always looked like he was watching a basketball game. I realized later he was right. Even when I brought my parents to the Western Wall in the Jewish Quarter in Jerusalem's Old City—my mother cried when she saw the tiny notes stuffed in the cracks of the wall—my father did look as though he was watching basketball. Observant yet mildly detached. A good game though. Maybe the end of a Bulls game in 1992 when Michael Jordan was at his best.

For years my mother talked about the yellow flowers I held in my hands and extended out to her as they exited the double doors into the warm, humid Mediterranean air. "They were so bright," she still says to me. I don't know why that detail stuck with her. Other people who were there to greet their loved ones also carried flowers. I certainly wasn't the only one. I think they were tulips. I can't remember. I was 24 in 1994. I had been studying for my Master's Degree in Literature at Hebrew University since 1992. My parents were 52—the age I am now—when they came to visit me for 10 days. I think the yellow tulips I carried and the wide purple and green paisley cotton pants I wore somehow solidified for my mother that I was really living in Israel. Up until that moment when she saw me standing there as she exited the double doors, my life in Israel was abstract to her. "My daughter is studying for her master's degree in Jerusalem!" she'd brag to her friends, but it must have sounded distant and exotic. So when she saw me in the crowd of people who lived there, waiting for the tourists who didn't live there to exit the double doors, still holding their passports because they hadn't had time yet to put them away, I really did look like I lived there. My dark brown hair was much lighter, too, from all the sun, she told me in the sherut. It must have been difficult for her. I had gone from living in their house during the weeks after graduating from college to living in another country with a very different life.

"Where did you get these flowers?" she asked me, smelling the tips. I explained that I got them from a guy near my apartment. "He's got flowers and vegetables and fruit. Just steps away," I said, as though I had lived there all my life. "It's not like in the U.S. where you have to drive to the grocery store like you do," I bragged.

My mother was right that the flowers were a symbol. When I had traveled with my parents to other places over the years we never bought flowers. Buying flowers is something you do when you're home. You bring them home from the store in a bag with a few other things and you cut the stems on the kitchen counter next to the sink and you make a mess before placing them in an old vase you take out from a cabinet of other older vases. You have too many vases. You should get rid of some of them. Most of them look alike anyway, especially the wide clear-glass ones. I didn't have a vase in Jerusalem, but giving my mother flowers in Israel told her I was home. "And these pants," she said, touching the purple and green paisley fabric. I told her they were comfortable in the hot Israeli weather. I knew how to dress in the Middle East. The elastic waist was the way to go, I explained. The wide legs were billowy and flowy. Wearing them made me look at ease. A real go-with-the-flow kind of girl. Except that I wasn't this kind of girl at all. I was anxious and nervous much of the time, worried about what people thought of me, including my parents, concerned when I was changing and growing beyond myself that no one would stick around. Looking back, I believe some of my anxiety stems from being attuned to social injustices at an early age, to feeling an unjust system, observing the mistreatment of others before I had language to name it.

It turns out this anxiety seems to be my natural state. At the time, the pants and other flowy and thin-fabric dresses and tops I bargained for in the shuk were like costumes I wore around Jerusalem, a city where I could pretend to be a laid-back hippy Jewish girl with long hair and wide billowy pants I had bargained for in the Arab market. I had seen other young women wear these kinds of pants when I'd first arrived, and I didn't know where they got them. These were the American Jewish girls who knew all the Israeli folk dances at the overnight Jewish summer camp I went to in Michigan. They looked light and breezy. They jumped and sashayed like ballerinas. They were airy, never heavy. They wore those pants. They fooled around with good looking guys in the tents we slept in. These were good Jewish girls, too. They loved Israel and sex. Years later, when I told my husband about these girls, he replied that these are the kinds of girls who have Daddy issues. "They're pretty with good skin, and they have damp, pouty lips and they're really smart and crazy," he said with a confidence of having known several. "Many of them go to Oberlin or Smith and major in Women and Gender Studies," he said.

In time I learned where to get the pants. First, you start calling the Arab market the shuk because that's what it's called. Second, you start bargaining with the Palestinian shop owner. When you ask him how much the pants cost, he says ten dollars and you say six and he says eight and you say seven. It feels like a game because you haven't yet realized that selling these pants is his livelihood. After you say seven you say, "Or I'll walk away," and you turn your face from him and then you turn your torso and you start to take a step away—part of the game is that you must look like you're serious—until he says okay, and then you turn back towards him, and the whole time you think you're just playing the game and you're glad that you learned how to play the game because maybe now you'll be like the light and breezy laid-back hippy good Jewish girls with long hair and wide billowy pants. You buy the pants for five and brag to your parents when they visit you. It's the first time you've seen them in over a year. They can't believe they used to see you every day. You meet them at the airport wearing the purple and green paisley wide cotton pants and you carry the bright yellow tulips and you know that despite the eleven-hour flight and despite your dad looking like he's watching a basketball game—"but a good game"—as he exits the double doors with the tourists, that they are so very, very happy to see you. "My sweet daughter," my mother says as she hugs me and sniffs my lightened hair, the yellow flowers between us.

I had reserved a room for them at the Kings Hotel on King George Street near Agron and Ramban Streets, a 10-minute walk from my apartment, which was on Chopin Street, just across from the Jerusalem Theatre. In the evenings, once they were in for the night, I smoked cigarettes and got high back at my apartment with my friend Danny, who was also studying for his master's degree at Hebrew University. On their third night in Jerusalem, they treated Danny and me to dinner at Mamma Mia, a popular Italian restaurant on King George Street. We each got a margherita pizza and my father joked that a can of Diet Coke was more expensive than a glass of wine and that you had to ask for ice. It was later that night when Danny said my father always looked like he was watching a basketball game. "Good seats," Danny said when we were stoned at my apartment. "Not courtside, but really good seats. He's always into the game."

During the 10 days they visited, my father read Philip Roth's 1993 *Operation Shylock* when he was resting in the hotel room. He had brought the hardback from Chicago. The novel follows the narrator, also named Philip Roth, to Israel where he finds his doppelganger, a man who spreads Diasporism, a non-Zionist ideology that advocates the return of Israeli Jews to their European homeland. I didn't have a doppelganger spreading a non-Zionist ideology in Jerusalem like the character in Roth's book, but sometimes I feel as though I might as well have because I grew into different versions of myself during the years I lived there. I don't remember my father talking about the book on that trip, but now I wish I had asked him about it and whether it challenged the Zionist beliefs he and my mother held, the same views I shared with them.

"I do not see any difference between Zionism and Judaism," my mother told me many times, once I was back in Chicago, when I tried to explain to her that I was changing. "I think there's more to Israel than I thought," I declared. "They were there, and I didn't know they were there. It wasn't an empty desert. Palestinians were there, and we mistreated them in our name," I said. Ironically, it was the values I was taught by my parents as a child—to care for others and to fight for justice—taken to their logical conclusion that caused me to eventually leave Zionism. "But you raised me to look at the world with a social justice lens," I tried to explain. But at the time, she couldn't hear it because it threatened her view of Israel, the Israel she needed to long for, the one that I, too, had longed for.

When I arrived in Jerusalem for graduate school it was there, in Jerusalem, walking on the cobblestones, where I consummated the love for the city I had developed as a little girl, staring at photos of it on my bedroom wall in Chicago, drawing pictures of it, creating giant maps of the country out of ice cream at camp. It was there, in Jerusalem, where the light hit the stone of the city walls and turned it golden and pink rose in the early mornings and again in the late afternoon. There, in Jerusalem, the smells of olives and za'atar and lemon and mint wafted through the corridors of the Old City.

And then one day, I became curious about the part of the Old City I had not visited. I walked from West Jerusalem to the Palestinian neighborhoods in East Jerusalem and I began making small talk with some of the Palestinian shop owners, then began spending time with them and listening to their stories. "How odd the two societies are not more integrated," I mused one time at a Palestinian spice shop in the shuk. The owner, Rami, laughed at me because I didn't yet understand that the system was deliberately set up so that Israelis and Palestinians wouldn't integrate, and that there was a terrible imbalance. I kept going back and met more Palestinians and listened to their stories, too. My Jewish friends in West Jerusalem told me that I was becoming a traitor, that I was "cavorting with the enemy." I tried to explain to them that they were wrong.

I don't know if I can describe the feeling that arrives when you realize that what you used to believe you no longer believe. It's a feeling that can make you nauseous and unsteady. Later, you realize some of the nausea was because you had an existential crisis. I kept going back, and deeper, too, beyond East Jerusalem, into Palestinian villages in the West Bank. Decades later, I realized that simply spending time in these areas and getting to know Palestinian people was enough to turn me into a bad Jewish girl. When you're a good Jewish girl, you're taught to stay away from these neighborhoods. You've been told by everyone around you that they are dangerous (the "enemy"), and that bad people live there. This included Damascus Gate, on the Northern side of the Old City, an area that is a center of Palestinian cultural life. If you're a good Jewish girl, you know that you should only enter at Jaffa Gate, on the Western side of the Old City, which you can take directly into the Jewish Quarter. You can get to the entrance of the shuk easily from Jaffa Gate, too. Today, promenades exist where people gather and visit, areas that seamlessly connect Jaffa Gate to West Jerusalem, further strengthening Israel's claim to the Old City.

Once I began spending time in East Jerusalem and ventured deeper in the West Bank, I began reading about Israel and Palestine, trying to understand what I had experienced, giving my mind a chance to catch up with my body. When I read Edward Said's 1979 essay, "Zionism From the Standpoint of its Victims," a friend said I was reading a terrorist. Yet in his essay, Said does more than my community did. I was never around Jews growing up who expressed a Palestinian point of view. Instead, I was told they did not exist. In his essay, Said sees how much Israel means to Jews, despite what it has meant for Palestinians. Not only does he present Zionism from the standpoint of its victims, he also understands Zionism from the standpoint of Zionists. "I know as well as any educated non-Jew can know, what anti-Semitism has meant for the Jews, especially in this century," Said writes. "Consequently I can understand the intertwined terror and the exaltation out of which Zionism has been nourished, and I think I can at least grasp the meaning of Israel for Jews." But Said can "also see and feel other things," he continues, "that complicate matters considerably, that cause me also to focus on Zionism's *other* aspects." Once I saw Zionism from the standpoint of its victims, as Said presents it, it was as though my eyes had come into focus after a lifetime of blurry vision.

"But Said is Palestinian, so he's biased," my Jewish friends told me. So I read Ilan Pappe's *Ethnic Cleansing of Palestine*, an Israeli. "He's Israeli and has similar views," I told them. "Pappe spent an enormous amount of time in the Israeli archives gathering his research," I told them. "But he left Israel," they stabbed back. "He's self-hating," they said. "He's anti-Semitic," they said. The friendships, of course, would soon end. But in the demise of these relationships, I realized the impossibility of competing with a myth. I eventually understood that nothing I ever said would have changed the minds of most of the people in my community. Things are different today. Jewish communities in the US are fed up with Israeli politics shifting to the right, and with Israel's mistreatment of its Palestinian population. I believe people are capable of great change, but it takes time. More young Jews are curious about Palestinian history and speak about it openly.

Yet at the time, reading these books made me sick, because I learned that there had always been books about Palestine, there had always been people writing and talking about Palestine, and what does it say about my community that the word Palestine or Palestinian and all these books written about Palestinian history never came up? Was my origin story also a myth if the stories I was told left out so many crucial details? I loved being Jewish, and so it became crucial that I find my own way out of Zionism through my Jewish identity, that I decide what had to be discarded and what could be preserved as most vital to my identity.

    A couple months before my parents' visit, at Jerusalem's Damascus Gate, while drinking tea at a Palestinian cafe, I met Salim and slowly came to understand that I knew really nothing at all about this city I had been in love with. I didn't mention Salim during my parents' visit. The night they left, after waving goodbye to them from outside the sherut, I walked past the front desk in the lobby, ignored the odd stare from the guy behind the desk, opened the door to the hotel room with my father's key, called Salim from the hotel room phone, and invited him over. I had eaten an early dinner with my parents around 4:00 pm. They set their alarm for midnight so they could get a few hours of sleep before the long trip back to Chicago. I slept on the floor of their room so I could be there with them when they left. The sherut picked them up at 1:00 am. The sheets were still warm from my parents, who had been able to sneak a few hours of sleep. So I guess, if we're really picking this scene apart, the sheets smelled like the four of us, once Salim and I went into the bed. We were gone before the 11:00 am checkout. We walked past the front desk and didn't stop because my father had already checked out the night before.

    Looking back now, it's clear there was much more happening that night than I realized, more than my acting out the night my parents left. Perhaps it was an unconscious power play on my part to invite a Palestinian to the hotel after my parents left. I'm sure Salim knew the risk of coming to a West Jerusalem hotel from East Jerusalem—what a person at times will do for sex!—so perhaps he didn't mind. Yet given what would happen later during my time with Salim—later, when he would be picked up by Israeli police outside a bar in Jerusalem, and even later, when he would be thrown in jail—I imagine that Salim was quite aware of the risk of coming to see me not in my apartment in West Jerusalem, which he had done many times, but in an Israeli-run hotel. Though I was a woman, I was more protected than Salim, and I had more power. I wonder now if sharing my parents' sheets with him—we wrapped ourselves with them playfully, like kids making a fort—was a way to yield some sort of power to him. But who knows? Maybe this is just my distorted way of making sense of the past, of the time when I was lonely and I fell in love, and crawled into their sheets because somehow I knew I'd already begun to separate from my parents.

A few days later, once my parents were settled back in Chicago, my father called me about an extra charge on his hotel bill. Apparently, he had also received a phone call from the reservations desk at the Kings Hotel telling him that a stranger had accompanied me to the room after they had left. I mumbled something about helping out a friend who happened to be near the hotel that night but we both knew it wasn't true. "What were you *thinking?*" my mother asked me, grabbing the phone from him. I didn't say. I also didn't tell them it was Salim. How quickly we regress when we are with our parents.

That night at the hotel was just the beginning of a rift between my parents and me. Over time, my understanding of Israel and Palestine would change. A distance would grow between us once I returned to Chicago, after completing my degree. It would take time for us to get close again. Inviting Salim was one data point in the story of becoming different from them in ways I was only beginning to understand. And it was just one story about shedding what it means to be a good Jewish girl, just one story of so many Jerusalem love stories that would end badly.

A JERUSALEM LOVE STORY GONE BAD:
SEARCHING FOR CIGARETTES IN JERUSALEM

Tavit and I met at Champs Bar in 1993, on Yoel Solomon Street right near Zion Square in downtown Jerusalem during the bar's Thursday dart night. He had thick, black, wavy hair, almond shaped eyes, and six-pack abs. The walls inside the bar were pocked and drizzled with gunshots from 1948, I was told, when Israel became a State. "Look closely," the bartender said, pointing just to the left of the dart board. "See those holes? That's the original wall." The bar was square-shaped and dark—the kind of lighting that made everyone look better than they did in natural light. It smelled of cigarette smoke and stale beer; Thursday nights brought in a familiar crowd. I remember one regular, Aryeh, who carried his darts and dart glove in his fanny pack every Thursday, and after getting his first drink, very carefully unzipped his fanny pack, placed it on the bar, and then methodically took out each dart and inspected the tips and wings of each one. Then he'd take out his dart glove and inspect that too. The bartender's name, fittingly, was Israel.

When I left Jerusalem after living there five years—and in love with Tavit for the last two—I waited for the taxi to take me to the airport. Tavit was with me. He's an Armenian Christian. "No one gives a shit about us here," he told me soon after we met. The Armenians are a subculture in Jerusalem, squeezed out by the dominant conflict. We'd been waiting for a quarter of an hour; the taxi would arrive any minute. We were on a busy road, Eshkol Boulevard—named for Levi Eshkol, Israel's fourth Prime Minister. I'd lived in so many different neighborhoods over the last five years: Rehavia, Katamon, downtown just off Ben Yehuda Street, and most recently, in Ramat Eshkol, a neighborhood next to French Hill and right near the university.

The Oslo years in Israel from 1993-1995 were seemingly hopeful. Israel and the PLO signed agreements designed to give Palestinians the right to self-determination. These agreements also created the Palestinian Authority, which gave Palestinians the ability to self-govern in parts of the West Bank and Gaza. Some of the more skeptical believed, however, that this gesture on Israel's part to give autonomy to the Palestinian Authority was only a facade of power, and that Oslo actually gave Israel more control over the Palestinian population registry. With this, Israel had the ability to collect data about Palestinians and to further monitor their movement. A Palestinian friend of mine, Hatem, would tell me stories of living in the West Bank city of Ramallah, unable to travel through the checkpoints to his parents who lived in Bethlehem. "It's a Swiss-cheese map," Hatem said, telling me about the checkpoints that dot the West Bank.

Since I was in Jerusalem on a student visa with a U.S. passport, I couldn't feel what this kind of monitoring must have been like for Palestinians, and under the pretense of peace. I wasn't Israeli either, so I didn't know what it was like to live with the constant threat of war. As an American Jew, though, I was naively hopeful for peace. I'd experienced several close calls with suicide bombings—just barely missing the number 23 bus that was targeted across the street from my apartment one morning during rush hour; I took it most days to the university but that particular morning I was hungover and sleeping—and felt a weird mixture of privilege and luck to have avoided all of the buses that blew up. I wanted peace and believed that those in charge wanted it too. When Prime Minister Rabin lit King Hussein's cigarette in 1994 minutes after they signed the peace treaty between Israel and Jordan, I carefully cut the photo out of Newsweek and taped it to my wall. "Peace pipe," the caption read.

While we waited for the taxi it became dark. I wasn't sure what time it was but I knew I called for the taxi to arrive at 9:00 pm. I didn't know if Tavit and I would see each other again. We hadn't really talked about it. Our relationship was full of smoking pot and having sex and talking about everything like old friends, just hanging out, like you do with someone when you're in your twenties. You don't really go on dates. You don't need a plan. You end a phone call saying, "Just come over and we'll figure it out," and you do. You go out somewhere or you don't, and if you do, you get there much later than you think you will because you've just been hanging out. That's how it was with Tavit. Our spending time together was more important than the things we did. This seems to be the opposite as I get older. Now, I make plans around doing something specific, like seeing a play, or going to a restaurant, or writing at the neighborhood cafe. I have a time limit on things I do now because I have to go to work the next morning and I'm tired. It's hard to remember a time—it's getting more difficult to even remember those years in my twenties when I lived in Jerusalem—when I just hung out.

One day when Tavit came over, he taught me how to make hummus. We didn't plan it, because I had told him to just come over. He was wearing my fuchsia shorts—we had just had sex—and I remember the smell of garlic on his hands from mashing it after we ate the hummus, and then had sex again. I smelled like garlic for days. You mash the chickpeas and garlic by hand, he told me. Never use a blender. Or when we he took me to the famous American Colony Hotel in East Jerusalem and we smoked and drank and pretended to be diplomats with grand ideas for world peace. I know that much of our hanging out was typical of our age, as I look back decades later, but from the start I knew that I was always leaving once I'd finished my studies in English and Hebrew Literature, and he was always staying in his home, Jerusalem, bound to marry an Armenian like him. His family has been in Jerusalem for the past 800 years, he told me, much longer than the Israelis and Palestinians, he joked, as he pointed out his family's home—also 800 years old—in the Armenian Quarter of Jerusalem's Old City. We didn't talk that much about what we would each do once I left. He'd keep working in his father's shop in East Jerusalem; I'd look for a job back in Chicago since I had completed my graduate studies.

After that first Thursday night dart night at Champs, we saw each other on several subsequent Thursdays and would talk a bit each time. After a few weeks, when he asked where I lived, ignorantly, I told him. The next night, around 11:00, he showed up to my apartment unannounced. When I opened the door, I saw that he looked upset. His nose was bleeding. His jeans were ripped and his knee was bloodied. He said he had gotten in a fight and didn't know where else to go. I asked him who hit him and he said some guys on the street in the Armenian Quarter in the Old City where he lived. Some Armenians, like Tavit's mother, have been in Jerusalem for centuries. Others who survived the 1915 genocide when the Ottomans killed 1.5 million Armenians, arrived after World War I. The Armenian Quarter is the smallest of the four—Christian, Jewish, and Muslim are the others—and often overlooked by outsiders who don't know its history. I had assumed his being beat up must have had something to do with the Israeli-Palestinian conflict. I had heard of attacks in the other quarters but I never heard anything about the Armenian Quarter.

I led Tavit into the bathroom. I motioned for him to sit on the toilet seat. I put some soap and water on a towel. I stood above him and cleaned the blood from his nose. He sat quietly and let me. I gave him the wet towel to press on his nose to stop the bleeding while I wiped the blood from his leg. I was a mother helping her son in some weird adult version of a tea party I'd hosted alone in my bedroom as a child. We were in a play no one was watching. We didn't talk. I put bandages on his nose and his knee. It was quiet outside. After, when the bleeding stopped, we walked into my bedroom and he lay down on my bed. The bed was in the corner of the room. Next to the bed were my bookshelves—three onion boxes on top of each other that I took from the grocery store around the corner from my apartment. I never bought bookshelves because I always knew I'd leave. Tavit knew he'd always stay. Two teal glass balls from the shuk hung in the window with white dental floss. I took his shoes off. We were both lying on our backs on the bed, looking up at the ceiling. I tried to give him more room by moving as close to the wall as I could. Periodically, I looked at him but I don't think he noticed. Soon he closed his eyes. I watched him sleep until I, too, fell asleep.

The next morning we woke up both facing the same direction away from the wall. My nose almost touched his back. He said he was embarrassed about the previous night. He asked if he could smoke in my bedroom. I said yes, and asked if I could smoke one of his cigarettes too. I offered to make some coffee and he said no, thank you, he had to go to work. He came back the next night, and the next, and for many nights after that. One night months later when we were talking and smoking and just hanging out, he brought up that first night he had come over unannounced. He said he hadn't gotten into a fight with some guys on the street near his home, but with his father, in his home. It was strange for me to be caring for Tavit in the apartment I had leased for one year—a temporary home at best—when he was unwelcome in his 800-year-old home. He said he didn't know where else to go. He thanked me for trusting him when he showed up (how ironic, I'll think later, that I, on a student visa, provided him with a home, and even more, the privilege I had to rent a home in a city closed off to so many Palestinians). He said he knew it was weird for him to come over like that. He would have understood, he told me, if I hadn't let him in.

He always finished his cigarettes before I did. I had always imagined putting the butts out in the ashtray together after sex, naked, dramatically, leaning with our elbows on the windowsill, our bare knees pushing into the mattress, after watching the smoke disappear. I would miss one night in particular when we stared out at the city, our clothes strewn all over the floor, and I watched him watch his city, and the way he would breathe in and then breathe out, like he had pressed a pause button on himself after a long day.

We did not have time to remain naked during my last night in Jerusalem, however, and I dressed quickly, anticipating the taxi that would soon arrive. That night seemed dreamy to me—a mix of pot smoking and crying. I knew what time my flight was but other than that I had no sense of time. Things seemed a bit blurry. I didn't realize it but I was starting to see those last moments with him as something in the past, looking back from the future, and it made me sad. My mind knew that the moment would soon become memory. I was already in between time and space, and soon, my body would catch up as I boarded the flight and physically went through time and space as I flew back to Chicago. My privilege to go back and forth between

Jerusalem and Chicago was lost on me. I wasn't yet aware of the political implications of my ability to travel within and outside of Israel with my U.S. passport when Palestinians are restricted within Israel and the West Bank.

One night Tavit picked me up from my apartment. We didn't know where to go. There had been another suicide bombing. This one was at a restaurant, Cheesecake, a few doors down from Champs on Yoel Solomon Street. Fourteen people were killed. Neither of us had been there, but we had both been close by. Tavit knew the family of the bomber. He was upset about the loss of life and also had empathy for the Palestinian man who detonated the bomb. He knew the hardships the family had living under occupation. Tavit held both sides in his heart in a city where people were polarized. After picking me up in Ramat Eshkol, Tavit drove towards the Old City. He went on Hebron Road, past the Cinematheque, then turned onto a quiet road with a steep incline—I can't remember the name now—with a view of the walls of the Old City, and put the car in park. On this hill, we were just a bit above the Old City. We didn't speak much. Periodically, Tavit would point something out like, "See that tower over there? That's part of the Armenian church." Or, "See that shop over there, just behind that part of the wall," he'd say, and light a cigarette in between his words, "the guy who owns it is such an asshole."

I watched him when he'd tell his stories; I'd watch him, too, when he was quiet. I had memorized the feelings associated with things he did: arching his eyebrows, laughing to a certain pitch, and recognizing pain in his voice on nights like this one when there had been a bombing. We sat in his car for a couple more hours. It was warm outside but we stayed inside as though we were at a drive-in movie watching an old show. I knew Tavit needed some distance from the only home he knew. The view of the Old City from his car, for me, was slightly similar to a photo of it that my mother gave me when I was a girl in Chicago. I had spent years staring at that photo of the Old City, taped to my teal bedroom wall, dreaming of visiting.

Tavit's home had become my playground. That we loved each other so deeply was framed by knowing we'd have no future. It could go deep because it was finite. I didn't think about my future too much but I knew he wouldn't be a part of it. I got sleepy that night in his car. On the short drive back home to my apartment, I dozed while Tavit drove, and knew he'd wake me up at home. He'd driven me around the city like a father whose daughter is asleep in the car with no worries about getting home safely.

I think that maybe from the outside we looked like an Edward Hopper painting that last night in Jerusalem. "Pink Bedroom (Window Seat)" might be the one. The man is sitting on the bed with his hand on the back of his neck. He's looking down. It seems like maybe he's just gotten dressed. The woman is sitting on the window seat looking out. The messy, loose white sheet on the bed indicates some sort of intimacy. The soft pinks and greens make it seem like it might be early morning. And like all Hopper paintings, there's a sadness and loneliness captured in the moment—like the moment is about to be over, but it lingers nonetheless, and for right now, it is heavy and full.

That night, as we dressed, Tavit sat on the bed like the man in the painting. I put on the same clothes I had worn for two days—dark blue Levi's and a maroon ribbed long-sleeve top—the only clothes I had not packed or shipped home. I wore them for three more days when I got to Chicago. I wouldn't shower because once I did, I knew the smell of him and Jerusalem would be gone from me. My mother, just diagnosed with breast cancer for what would be the first of three times in 20 years, would say to me, "Honey, please, take a shower. You'll feel better." For weeks after returning, when no one was looking, I'd look at the clock, then count up eight on my fingers so that I'd know what time it was in Jerusalem.

For years, I convinced myself that I'd be happier in that other time zone, my mind and body disjointed, a series of "if only this or that," repeated in my head, as my dad threw the job ads at me at breakfast. With each day that passed I'd feel more distant from Jerusalem and inevitably, what I just came home from would become memory, as my time in Jerusalem settled into a different part of my brain. Those memories eventually became nostalgia, and I started to misremember things.

Years later, when I do return, the city will be unrecognizable to me, ancient roads replaced with pedestrian malls made to look like they'd always been there. Champs will be long gone—a baby-clothes boutique in its stead—and I'll walk by and wonder who remembers. I'll become lost on Jaffa Road; sidewalks will have disappeared and there will be no traffic but a new tram down the center of the street. And when I see my mother aging over the years, radiation and mastectomies having caused deeper lines in her face, I'll remember the love she extended to me when I returned, lost, in 1995, a self-absorbed twenty-five year old—holding me like a baby when I didn't know what to do with my culture shock while she was sick.

A cab drove by. It wasn't the one. I looked at Tavit when he looked away. I compared the angle of his chin to the hills behind Jerusalem and I noticed how it aligned perfectly with the hills outlined by the lights in the distance. In that second I couldn't separate my love for Tavit from my love for Jerusalem. It was cool outside. The next morning I knew it would be hot and the hills would be so white with sand and stone they'd be blinding. When I returned years later, the hills I had compared Tavit's chin to—who was I to compare a face to a landscape, anyway?—would no longer just be hills, but would have an entirely new landscape of settlements and concrete walls.

And when I see him 22 years later, when we're both 45, Tavit and I will have aged as well. We'll both be married. He'll have married an Armenian and have three kids. He'll drive me to Bethlehem to visit some friends. As we exit Bethlehem and go through the checkpoint near Rachel's Tomb, the entire city surrounded by an apartheid wall, he'll say, "There's no money in peace." We'll both notice the soldier at the checkpoint flirting with the Palestinian woman who's in her car trying to get through. She'll bat her eyelashes and smile at the soldier, and hope for the soldier's weakness. We'll laugh about it though it's not funny. I'll tear up as we say goodbye, not knowing when I'll see him again, confused by age and my distorted memories of Tavit and Jerusalem. Through my tears, I'll remind him of one of the letters he sent me when I was back in Chicago in 1995 and he suggested we meet in Italy the next summer. "Why didn't we ever do that?" I asked him as he wiped the tears from eyes and kissed my forehead. He didn't know.

For a moment, in my mind, seeing him again will become some kind of a marker in my life. I'll say to friends when I get home, "And then I saw him 22 years later…" as if seeing an old lover when one has aged has some sort of significance I cannot name. Like a teenager, I'll ask him when we hug goodbye, if we'll always be friends—I won't have used that expression in decades—as though his answer, "Yes, of course," will somehow make it so. I don't know if that will happen.

I won't want to say goodbye, so I'll do what I did 25 years ago and suggest we smoke cigarettes. In my mind, I do the math and think if we smoke five more, each one will take five minutes, and that will mean at least 25 more minutes together. We sit on a bench near the front of my hotel and ash our cigarettes and throw the butts on the ground. My lungs will hurt in the morning. I'm too old for this. I fear I don't fit in anywhere. The next morning, I'll leave the hotel. It's hot outside. Once I've exited the building, I'll walk over to the bench where we sat. Several kids run around it. I won't feel like being in the sun. In a few hours, I'll head to the airport. The last letter I received from Tavit in 1995 after I returned to Chicago said, "I really miss the days we had together in Jerusalem. I think we'll see each other someday, somewhere, and it will be even nicer. I think the older we get the better we will be." I'll insist the taxi driver take Highway 1 instead of Road 443 so I can take my time. As I leave Jerusalem again, I'll want to feel the slow descent. But before I go, I walk around the bench searching for cigarette butts to make sure Tavit and I were really there.

But during my last night in Jerusalem, though, at age 24, I didn't distinguish between my love for him from my love for the city. Both the city and the lover had been a playground for me to explore like a new canvas—having had the gall to superimpose our young selves on a Hopper painting, of all things! As we waited outside for the taxi, I thought that I might be able to laugh at myself, for I knew that last night had become so dramatic. It would be so funny, I thought at the time, if we could laugh about this tomorrow when we go get something to eat but then I remembered that we wouldn't do that.

The cab finally came and I got inside. I didn't look back, though I knew Tavit had started to walk home. I looked ahead, and as it started to rain,

I stared through shiny wet glass that made all the lights of the city look bigger and brighter than they really were. The driver turned from Eshkol Boulevard beginning the descent to Highway 1 that took us down and out of Jerusalem towards the airport. The rain hit the windshield hard and it became difficult to see. My view of Jerusalem was distorted. It was fitting to leave it this way. From inside the taxi, I watched the city move, even though it was me who was moving. Jerusalem was still. It would stay that way for a little while.

Five days after I arrived back in Chicago, Prime Minister Yitzhak Rabin was assassinated by the right-wing Jewish Israeli extremist Yigal Amir. The hope for peace ended, and with it the hope—however idealistic—that the Oslo Accords would make a difference and bring peace and an end to the occupation. Settlement expansion would increase, as would Israeli and Palestinian frustration. A few days after Rabin's assassination I received a letter from Tavit, the first of several that arrived. After my first year back in Chicago, the letters stopped. I'll email him 22 years later telling him I'm coming to Jerusalem and ask if we can get together for coffee. "I don't think there will ever be peace," he wrote in the letter to me after Rabin's assassination. "Sometimes I don't think anyone wants peace." He wrote that because of recent violence, his father's shop and many shops in East Jerusalem have been closed for a while. "I don't know if we'll be able to reopen because the situation is so bad. I'll always be in Jerusalem in the same damn shop," he wrote. "Mark my words. Things will only get worse."

BRAVADO ON A HILL

During our breaks in between classes, my friend Danny and I would meet at our spot in the Botanic Gardens on Mt. Scopus, a six-acre garden founded by botanist Alexander Eig in 1931 just a few years after Hebrew University opened. The gardens has one of the largest collections of Israeli plants in the small country.

Danny and I had our favorite spot, a large flat rock near pink and yellow and lavender flowers. We'd gaze down at the bustle of the city, marvel at the outline of the wall wrapping around the Old City, and picture what it might have looked like thousands of years ago. Like children, we'd use our fingers and pretend we were holding little trucks and tanks, and move them around the city that seemed so tiny in between our hands, making little explosion noises as we crashed our imaginary tanks into each other.

Having gotten some distance, we'd soon return, descending from our spot on the hill to the city below. We came to our spot to gain a perspective of the city—really, our place in it—and to sit physically above and watch the buses—numbers 4A or 18 from downtown or 23 which went through East Jerusalem—wind around the streets and other hills below us. We were detached from the noise and dirt and commotion. We felt this way often on Mt. Scopus, attending graduate school on a hill, and we developed what I'd later recognize as a false sense of perspective because we were physically higher than others. Without making the connection, we had replicated what soldiers do—physically placing ourselves above the city, a timeless strategy used in military operations.

The distance gave us a proud frame of reference. We were in love with the city, and as young liberal Zionists, thought we had legitimate claim to the city we were using as our temporary home as graduate students. Often, our talks included dreams—distorted visions of our daily life—and we bragged how Jerusalem had leaked into our unconscious mind.

One day after our literary criticism seminar, we met at our spot and I told Danny I had recently had another Hamas dream. We had shared stories about such dreams before. Our sense of detached bravado in the city we lived in but didn't pay taxes or work full time, did, however, leak into our dreams. As dreams will, ours reflected our unconscious fears about living as students in a foreign land, unaware of the historical context around us.

"You and I were walking in the Jewish Quarter in the Old City again, right near the steps down to the Kotel," I told him. "And then in the dream Hamas would find us and chase us down the narrow streets and they'd catch us and kidnap us."

The first time we both talked about having that same Hamas dream was after a bombing in a Jerusalem restaurant on Yoel Solomon Street which was next door to a cafe where we had been having dinner. First we heard the loud explosion, then screams, and then we saw people running down Yoel Solomon Street. I remember seeing bullet holes in the bookstore Gur Arieh Books, where we often frequented. We left the cafe in a hurry and jumped into a taxi, smelling something burning and sour that must have been human flesh. The next day we met at our spot on the rock after our morning seminar (mine was Beckett; Danny's was Nietzsche). While we sat on our rock, we tried to find Yoel Solomon Street and the restaurant from where we were on the hill, as though locating it from a distance would help remove some of the trauma we had experienced the night before.

Growing up as liberal Zionists, persecution dreams were not new to us. As a child, I had similar Anne Frank in the attic dreams. I was obsessed with Anne Frank's story and would often dream of the Nazis coming to get me when I'd be sleeping. In 1978 when I learned about the Holocaust for the first time in Hebrew school, I came home and hid in the basement. My father, upon returning from dinner, asked me what I was doing when he saw me crouched behind a couch. "I'm hiding from the Nazis," I exclaimed. "Get upstairs for dinner," he balked. "And do your homework." The Hamas dreams Danny and I talked about were just another version, a kind of post-Holocaust, post-1948 Zionist dream.

The most recent shift in my dreams began once I started to question Zionism. A few years ago, I visited the West Bank on a solidarity trip with 20 other Jews. We stayed with Palestinians in Jenin and the Deheishe refugee camp in Bethlehem. The Palestinian family—Dima, Huba, Ahmed, Sami, Abu, and Abeha—in Deheishe had been living in the camp since its establishment in 1949, not uncommon for people who live in Deheishe.

After a lovely dinner and conversation, my hosts went to bed. I was staying in an added-on, square-shaped room on the roof of their home—one of the only ways for Palestinians who live in Deheishe to build and add needed space—when I started to remember the Hamas and Anne Frank in the attic dreams. I must have fallen asleep thinking of these, because I awoke from another, what I now call the Zionist Refugee Camp dream. In this dream, I am still a Jew frightened about being rounded up and taken. But this time I am a Jew worried that it's the Israeli soldiers barging in and taking me.

I awoke from the dream, confused at first about where I was, and then, minutes later, sickened at the newly-discovered privileged empathy for my hosts: to finally feel what they had been living as part of their day-to-day lives. What privilege that the real conditions of their lives came to me in a dream, and that I would leave Deheishe after a three-day visit and head back to a hotel in Jerusalem and take a hot shower. I got up that morning in the camp, ate a delicious meal of pita and hummus, baba ganoush, tahini, and other salads set out by my host. I didn't mention the dream.

But at age 25, shortly before we both left Jerusalem with our master's degrees in our hands, Hebrew University blocked off the entrance to the Botanic Gardens to rebuild some of the gardens. Unable any longer to sit on our rock and gain the perspective we thought we needed (and could only get on top of the hill), we made our way down to the city, the dust and dirt from the buses and roads hitting us in our faces as we walked towards the bus stop.

THE STAMP COLLECTOR

I think the first stamps my father ever gave me were of Jim Henson surrounded by The Muppets. The sheet was a special issue in the 1980s when The Muppets were on TV from 1976-1981. I didn't understand why he gave it to me and I didn't know what to do with it. I wondered why he couldn't have gotten me something more tangible I could play with, like Kermit's guitar—I had asked for one for Hanukkah—for Kermit to hold when I'd have him sing "The Rainbow Connection" from *The Muppet Movie,* which I saw four times the year it was released, in 1979. He never explained why he gave me the stamps. Being my father's daughter, I've learned not to ask. Some things just don't need to be talked about.

When I was in college, I told my father I was interested in Peace Studies. He laughed and said I'd never find a job. The following summer I was living at home and bartending, and when I came home late one night from the bar, I saw several World Peace stamps from St. Vincent and the Grenadines in the Caribbean on the kitchen table. A set of three, they featured Gandhi, Elie Wiesel, and Rigoberta Menchu. He never brought it up. I put the stamps in my room with the others he's gotten me over the years.

A few days after going to a Renoir exhibit at the Art Institute in Chicago in 2008, my father presented me with a Renoir stamp of the painting

"La Femme Au Chat et La Fiancée" printed in Burundi. My parents have a copy of the Renoir painting framed at their house. I have a Marc Chagall stamp in Hebrew, Russian, and French from Belarus that was printed on the 125th anniversary of Chagall's birthday. I've several Edward Hopper stamps, including one from France of one of my favorite paintings, "Soleil du matin, 1952."

My father has been a philatelist since he was a kid. He's got thousands of stamps—some old and some new, but all rare. He'll often go to stamp shows, even ones hours away, stay half the day, make deals with other old guys, and come home with his new stamps delicately protected in plastic which he'll only remove with tweezers like he's performing surgery. The only other time I've seen him handle something so methodically is when he pulls sliced lox from its package on Saturday and Sunday mornings and places it carefully on his bagel, which he's already prepared with cream cheese. The best gift my mother ever gave him was a magnifying glass that sits by itself with a ledge where he can place his stamps to look at behind the glass without hands.

He's also a pediatrician, and a lover of the history of medicine. When he edited a medical journal for a couple decades, he wrote a feature article every month on stamps from his personal collection that related to the issue's particular theme. One issue includes stamps from Malaysia that illustrate various forms of malaria parasites. A 2011 stamp from Serbia highlights the need to "Stop Polio Now." A 1996 stamp from India illustrates the anatomy of the heart and celebrates 100 years of cardiac surgery. A 1987 stamp from Magyar, Hungary, shows the systemic and pulmonary circulations of the heart. A Spanish stamp from 2011 honors the 500th birthday of Miguel Servet, the first European to describe the function of the pulmonary circulation. The diabetes issue featured stamps from Oskar Minkowski (1858–1931), honored on a 1990 Transkei stamp highlighting a milestone in the conquest of diabetes. A Belgian stamp depicts insulin's positive reaction to sugar and its molecular structure. The AIDS issue features AIDS stamps from Bosnia-Herzegovina and Serbia.

When a 14-year-old Pakistani student of mine, Azan, was diagnosed with Thalassemia, a rare blood disorder, my father got me a stamp with a picture of the first child ever diagnosed with the disease. The stamp came from Pakistan and included the little perforations around it that are important to stamp collectors. The first postage stamps, available in Great Britain and Ireland in 1840, had to be cut from sheets with scissors until they were made with perforations a decade later. "You should frame the stamp," my father told me, "and give it to your student." For most of the school year, Azan was in the children's hospital where my father works. I told my father I wanted to visit him. I wasn't family, though, so I wasn't allowed to see him. "Come to the hospital," my father said. "I'll get you in. Briefly." I arrived at my father's office, and after instructing me to put on scrubs and gloves and a mask, he walked me to the section of the hospital where Azan was staying. He used his staff ID to open the door to the area, and told me to hurry up. I gave Azan the framed stamp. He started to cry. We wouldn't talk about it.

When Obama was elected president in 2008, my father bought me a mint sheet of stamps from Liberia that feature Obama's face. I've got the first stamps ever issued with Anne Frank's name and picture. It accompanies the stamp he got me with Miep Gies, the woman who helped hide the Franks in Amsterdam. The stamp is a "First Day Issue" on an envelope signed by Gies. He included the certificate of authenticity that came with it when he gave it to me. "So you know it's legit," he said. I have three Shakespeare stamps from Gibraltar: each with a quote from *Hamlet, Midsummer Night's Dream,* and *Macbeth* he gave me when I started teaching high school English in 2003. When I met my husband Tony, I wasn't sure my father would like him. "He's not Jewish," I told him when we started dating, "and he's a poet." We didn't talk about it. After we got married, my father bought my husband five stamps, each a favorite poet of Tony's (I think my mother sneakily told him who they were): Gwendolyn Brooks, William Carlos Williams, Sylvia Plath, Elizabeth Bishop, Denise Levertov. "You should frame them," he told me, "and give them to Tony."

Perhaps my father is so cerebral because he's a scientist and a researcher. But he's got the best bedside manner of any doctor I know, and his patients love him. Too much emotion just isn't his thing. Or maybe it's because he was seven years old when his dad died. His father survived World War II on a ship in the Pacific only to come home and die of cancer a few years later. I think of that when I remember being a bratty 12-year-old preparing for my Bat-Mitzvah, and he told me I had to keep practicing in front of him. He was editing an article he wrote and didn't look up. I'd chant my haftorah portion, and when I finished, he'd say, "Again." After chanting it four times, I blurted out, "I bet your dad didn't force you to practice like this." He said, "My father was dead when I prepared for my Bar-Mitzvah." I continued to chant.

Though I had given up on majoring in Peace Studies in college and had decided to double major in English and Hebrew—that decision elicited the same concern from my father about my future ability to find a job—I decided I wanted to study abroad in Israel my junior year. I was accepted to Tel-Aviv University. It was fall 1991. The world was building up to first Gulf War; my father said I couldn't go. A week later, he gave me a set of stamps with the founders of Israel, and another Israeli stamp with the word peace in English, Hebrew, and Arabic. We didn't talk about it. One morning at breakfast over bagels he told me that the first stamps in Israel were issued two days after Israel became a state in 1948.

I did finally get to Israel for school. Hebrew University in Jerusalem was the only graduate school I applied to in 1992 (again, for English and Hebrew Literature). When I got accepted, I bought a duffel bag and a one-way ticket to a program I didn't know much about. I returned to Chicago in 1995, five days before Yitzhak Rabin was assassinated. A couple months after the assassination, my father got his hands on a First Day Issue from the Federated States of Micronesia with Yitzhak Rabin on it. Rabin's name and dates of his birth and death were printed on the stamp, along with "Peacemaker, Prime Minister of Israel." The other two countries to issue a stamp honoring Rabin were Israel and The Republic of the Marshall Islands.

Israel's stamp came out 30 days after Rabin's assassination in observance of Shloshim, a memorial held on the 30th day after someone has died, for the first time in Israel's history. Stamps usually take months to design and produce, so it was rare for the stamp to come out in a month. When John

F. Kennedy was killed, for example, the U.S. Postal Service issued its memorial stamp seven months later. When Rabin was assassinated in 1995, stamp printers were able to produce stamps more quickly. I've also got a five-shekel Rabin stamp that came out after the original memorial stamp. It says, "Prime Minister and Minister of Defense, 1922-1995." Ten years later, in November of 2005, my father gave me a sheet of nine stamps celebrating the opening of the Yitzhak Rabin Center in Tel-Aviv, designed by the Israeli architect, Moshe Safdie. The stamps were issued on the tenth anniversary of Rabin's assassination.

A couple months before Rabin was killed, I was able to reverse our tradition. After all the years of him giving me stamps, I was able to buy him one. I got him the First Day Issue celebrating 3000 years of Jerusalem's City of David. The year 1996 (5756-57) was to be declared the "Tri Millennium of Jerusalem, the City of David." I sent him an email on September 4, 1995, soon after I got the stamp:

Dad—Today the post office issued new stamps marking the 3000th anniversary of Jerusalem. I got you a bunch, and yes, they have the perforations. They're really beautiful, old pictures of Jerusalem, plus one of the Knesset. I'll bring them home with me. I got up really early today to get them because they only made a certain amount.

It was the least I could do. I look back on this pattern that developed over the years with tenderness. Rather than express much emotion, my father acknowledged different aspects of my identity through stamps. That I got him one didn't change the dynamic that it was really his hobby; I had simply entered his world for one day. It was a perfect situation: Dad doesn't have to talk; daughter gets recognition. He can be who he is and I can be who I am. Instead of messy expectations and limitations, it was a clean nonverbal agreement we had. It worked. It was unique just to us. I felt like he really *saw* me when he gave me a stamp. Like, without words he was saying, *I know what your interests are and who you are and what you value, and I like it.*

I wish this could be the end of the story, that it could have stayed just like this. It'd certainly be a precious ending to a personal essay about a father's love for a daughter as shown through stamps. But things couldn't stay this way. Everything changes. Marrying a Buddhist—I haven't gotten a stamp about *that* yet—has helped me to understand that everything is always changing. In his book, *What Makes You Not a Buddhist*, Dzongsar Jamyang Khyentse talks about change as inevitable. "Everything must change," he writes, "because everything is interdependent, everything is subject to change." Khyentse explains:

> If you feel hopeless, remember this and you will no longer have a reason to be hopeless, because whatever is causing you to despair will also change. Everything must change.

I often think of this quote as I'm getting older, teaching in the world of public education—I taught English and Hebrew in my first teaching job, squashing my father's worry about what job I'd get—which has become more corporatized with massive budget constraints. "If you are enjoying a cup of tea," Khyentse writes, "and you understand the bitter and the sweet of temporary things, you will really enjoy the cup of tea." As I began to learn about the Palestinian narrative for the first time, my new awareness became interdependent and intertwined, and inevitable, really, with my love for Jerusalem. Things got a bit tricky. Everything about my relationship to Israel—and to my father—was changing.

I was shocked at what I discovered as I began studying Palestinian history: that the land hadn't been empty as I had been told growing up; that conditions for Palestinians in the West Bank and Gaza were horrific; that the current occupation was a direct result of what had happened in 1948 and again in 1967; that Israel professed to the world that it wanted peace and I had believed that it was true, but it wasn't true at all; and that Zionism wasn't the same as Judaism. Most of all, I was angry that I had believed the narrative I was taught growing up. And I felt shame at finally learning about it when I did, like I had some epiphany about Palestine that so many others already knew about. I'd meet other activists who grew up reading Edward Said and criticizing Zionism, and I felt behind. Looking back, with the worldview I have now, it seems impossible that I didn't know. All the people and books and history existed. To continue learning about Palestine, I realized, would mean I'd have to undo what I had learned. I didn't see this as a choice; I couldn't turn back.

The first Palestinian stamps issued were a result of the Oslo Accords. After the Cairo Peace Agreement was signed in 1994, the Palestinian Authority took over post offices in Gaza and Jericho. In 1995, the Palestinian Authority had control of post offices in the West Bank; their stamps could be used within Israel and internationally. Gaza had its own stamps in 2009 that were used locally. When Hamas and Palestinian Authority governments in Gaza and the West Bank unified in 2014, Gaza stamps could be used on all Palestinian Authority mail. The stamps issued, of course, were Palestine's desire to show its nationhood, as other nations have done, despite the infighting among its different factions. The stamps are simply representations of ideas, government-sponsored attempts to establish a history. The idea of Israel that I grew up with had become different than its reality. And as I learned more about the Palestinians, the idea of Palestine—a people without a state—became more real. "Stamps are excellent primary sources for the symbolic messages governments seek to convey to their citizens and to the world," stamp historian Donald M. Reid has written. Stamps help legitimize a country, amalgamate an idea that may or may not be different from the reality.

As I learned more about Palestine, I stopped receiving stamps from my father. I already wasn't getting any verbal recognition, which I was okay with when I got the stamps *because I got the stamps*, but now I wasn't receiving stamps *or* words. Later, I'd understand that my shift from Zionist to anti-Zionist thinking must have been very confusing for my father. I had moved to Israel an ardent Zionist, and then later, developed an unwavering criticism of Israel that involved trips to Palestine—I starting calling it Palestine—to work with Palestinians and other Israelis who would also criticize Israel's policies. I'd scoff at the JUF newspaper my parents received. I used to read it religiously. My stamps sat in a box.

By now, you know that when I say I stopped receiving stamps, what I'm really saying is that my father stopped *seeing* me. I was doing other things, of course, like teaching and traveling and dating. It's not like I was sitting around thinking about Israel and Palestine all day. Well, actually, I was. Once my feelings started changing about the unconditional love I used to hold for Israel, it permeated everything else. And my father wasn't the only one confused. Men I dated were confused too. I had joined JDate when I was in love with Israel. I got in arguments with guys I met on the site if they hadn't visited the country. I wanted to talk about it more than anything else. An ex-boyfriend, Mark, whom I dated when I was a Zionist, had enough of it one day. "Israel, Israel, Israel, it's all you ever talk about," he yelled. I replied, "I can't believe you haven't been there." We broke up soon after. When I was on JDate and was no longer a Zionist, I fought with guys about that too. I'd get angry if men I met on JDate hadn't been there *and* weren't criticizing Israel enough. More than anything, though, I worried that my relationship with my father had been conditional; I had to like what he liked in order to be seen. It hurt and I worried that he just didn't like me.

During the period I wasn't receiving stamps, I'd miss my younger self—long before I learned about ideas and their true or false representations of reality—and I'd get upset about things like wanting more Muppet paraphernalia. I remember in 1990 when my father asked to borrow my Kermit the Frog and Miss Piggy stuffed animals. He was giving a lecture, he said, and wanted them for the slideshow that would accompany his talk. It took me a while but I found them in the attic. When I asked him why he needed my beloved animals, he said the lecture was on streptococcal toxic shock syndrome. This meant nothing to me—a 20-year-old studying literature—and I watched him, dumbfounded, as he spent an hour posing my favorite Hollywood couple on the kitchen table late at night. They were dusty, and years before, I had cut Miss Piggy's hair and gave her a mole on her cheek with a black sharpie. My father didn't seem to mind. I remembered, as I watched him meticulously getting the right shot for his slide, when I was younger and alone and I'd pose Kermit and Miss Piggy in various sexual positions, and here was my father, posing them for a medical lecture. Perhaps he missed his younger self too. When I asked, he told me that Jim Henson died of streptococcal toxic shock syndrome.

Later, it happened. It just did, I don't know why. I came home late one night and on the kitchen table were several Palestinian stamps. The gesture didn't mean he supported the Palestinian Authority, or even Palestine. Rather, it was his way of showing interest in my political shift by giving me the only Palestinian stamps he could find. It was an affirmation of an idea that was important to me. A First Day Issue from 1998 had ancient drawings of the Dome of the Rock in Jerusalem. Another was the stamp of Arafat and Clinton signing the Oslo Accords in 1998 at the Wye River Conference. A 1998 First Day Issue showed a light brown and yellow mosaic floor of a Byzantium Church. A set of five Palestinian Authority stamps featured herbs and fruit on each stamp: lemon, poppy, orange, thyme, and hibiscus. The stamps were brilliant shades of yellow and pink and red and orange and green. A small blue post-it next to the stamps said, "Liz."

Stamps are nothing more than a nation's accepted ideas put onto sticky paper. For many, Israel and Palestine have come to represent transient political constructs in whose name much reciprocal suffering is inflicted. And yet, the whole idea of a nation, for Palestinians, remains elusive and possibly out of reach. My father understood the bitter and the sweet of temporary things, and it made me sad. He was trying. We wouldn't talk about it, but we'd really enjoy the cup of tea.

But that was all a long time ago. Everything changes. And conditions have gotten worse in Palestine while American children play with their Muppets, posing their animals in odd positions, unaware yet of the world of ideas, waiting desperately for fathers who may or may not see them.

WHILE HE WAS STOPPED BY SOLDIERS: ANOTHER JERUSALEM LOVE STORY GONE BAD

The first hour of the drive to Eilat, the resort-town in Israel three hours south of Jerusalem was, in a way that I remember now, like a road trip movie: my feet propped up on the dashboard, my toes sticking out the window as Khalil drove. The wind blew our hair back. We had Diet Coke and potato chips. A week before, when Khalil asked me to drive to Eilat with him, I wondered if we'd hook up. Going to stay in a hotel could only mean one thing. But I didn't ask. I said yes, and packed one pink dress, a red skirt, one pair of brown sandals, and my teal bathing suit. I was young and confident. I had recently mastered the mass transit bus system in Jerusalem. I could get anywhere at any time and never had to ask anyone for directions. If, on the rare occasion I didn't know, I'd use my Hebrew to ask. When strangers on the street asked me for directions, they asked me in Hebrew—a sure sign that I was looking less American and more Israeli. I was 21, living abroad in Jerusalem as a graduate student, and I sported an overly confident attitude about things I knew nothing about.

Khalil was 21, too, and we had met at a cafe near the Jaffa Gate in Jerusalem months before we drove to Eilat. This cafe served mostly tourists, but Khalil and I had been in Jerusalem almost a year already, and we began talking by scoffing at those we could tell were visiting for just a week or so. We sat at white plastic tables on red plastic chairs. The smells of za'atar and sumac floated around us when we spoke. The first thing I noticed about him was his necklace, a gold state of Palestine. It was the first time I saw what I was taught was the map of Israel, with city names in Arabic. I looked at his necklace against his brown skin and clutched my own necklace, a modern gold chai, the Hebrew word for "life," and the lucky number eighteen, too, the legs bowed at the top and then narrowed. Khalil is a Palestinian-American, the youngest and only child of seven to be born in the U.S. with all the others born in Palestine. After growing up in the U.S. and graduating college, he had come to Palestine to live in Ramallah with an older brother for a year. For Khalil, hanging out in Jerusalem came to be a Westernized respite from living with his family under occupation in Ramallah. For me, going to cafes and bars in Jerusalem were small breaks from my evening graduate seminars at Hebrew University. At first, we ran into each other at the cafe a few times. After several weeks, we started to hang out more. A month later, he asked me to drive to Eilat for the weekend. I didn't bother to ask if we'd have separate hotel rooms. We'd just figure it out.

Once we had been on the road for a while, I noticed a siren behind us. I figured—in my naïveté, I realize now—that Khalil must have been speeding. He wasn't. We were pulled over by a car full of Israeli soldiers. They told Khalil to step out, forcing him to place his arms over his head and pushing him against the car. Using his knee, one of the soldiers spread Khalil's legs wide. The soldiers were handsome. One flirted with me while he looked through my U.S. passport as the others accosted Khalil. I smiled and clutched my chai necklace as the soldier looked through my passport. Khalil's passport was American, too, but that didn't help him as they searched his body. From inside the car, I watched them lift Khalil's shirt and look down his pants. While he was being frisked, I sat in the car wondering if we would have sex that weekend.

Another soldier looked like the Israeli soldier I met on my first trip to Israel at age 16. He had curly, dark hair and green eyes and a scruffy chin. I was dared by the other American Jews I was with—we were on a summer program—to kiss a soldier and ask him for the shirt of his Israeli army uniform. We made out for a minute against the wall of a bar in Jerusalem's Russian Compound as the other American teens cheered. I brought his shirt home with me, folded carefully in my suitcase, at the end of the summer program when I returned to Chicago. It was a perverse initiation into Zionism, I would learn, that many American Jewish girls go through. His M16 pressed against my leg while we kissed. As I watched the soldiers harass Khalil, I felt sick for playing in the charade when I was a teenager, for seeing what is oppressive for Palestinians as a rite of passage for American Jews.

After, Khalil got back in the car. The soldiers were done. He ran his fingers through his dark, thick hair, and turned to me. "That was fun," he joked. "I wanted to stop." He put his seatbelt on, shifting the car into drive. "How generous of the soldiers to give us a break while on the road," he said, feigning a smile. "It sure was nice of them," I replied, playing along as we drove south. He lit a cigarette. I pretended not to notice his trembling fingers as he smoked. Soon, I lit one too.

The hotel was fancy, big and yellow with lots of staff wearing crisp white. The lobby had round, pink chairs that looked like they were from the set of Mad Men, cozy to have drinks in. A big pool glistened in a bigger courtyard; each room had access to the pool. When we arrived, I stood behind Khalil as he approached the front desk. He asked for one room with two beds. He didn't look to me to see if this was ok. I was cool with whatever, I told myself.

Later that night, after eating dinner at a nearby restaurant—falafel, hummus, tahini with parsley, red wine, chicken and lamb kebabs that smelled like lemon and thyme—we lay on one of the beds in the hotel. Our stuff was on the other bed. Khalil was on his back and I was on my stomach next to him, my head resting against my arm. I was still unsure if we would have sex—it had not come up at all, or even why we decided to go to Eilat in the first place—and I ran my fingers through his hair, and he closed his eyes and breathed deeply for the first time all day. The room was quiet. I traced the shape of his eyebrows with my finger. I was glad he was resting after what had happened on the highway with the Israeli soldiers. He still hadn't talked about it, and I didn't bring it up. I listened to his breathing as his eyes remained closed. I felt like my mother when I was young, and she, sensing my upset, would rub my back and calm me down, and I would purr like a cat.

We didn't stay on the bed long. After a few minutes, as though sensing the softness and not wanting to remain in it, Khalil jumped up and said, "Let's go get a drink!" We walked to the lobby and sat in the big, pink chairs and drank fruity drinks with bananas and kiwi and rum with tiny, green umbrellas that teetered on the edge of the glass mugs filled with smashed ice. I asked Khalil about his family while we were drinking. "I mean, how does it feel to be the only one born in the U.S.?" I questioned him. "I don't know," he said. "I guess I'm just more Americanized than they are," he quipped as he sipped his drink. "I mean, if you came to stay in Ramallah with your brother," I said, "why are you hanging out so much in predominantly Jewish Israeli areas?" He couldn't answer. "Why, that's easy," he said. "The drinks are better on this side of the Green Line." He got us another drink; it was clear talking about identity just wasn't his thing.

Later, when we were returning to the hotel room, we walked by the pool to get back to our room. The water was blue like the Mediterranean Sea he said his family members in the West Bank are forbidden to visit. We were the only people around. I thought perhaps we might hold hands. What happened next surprised me. When we were just a few feet from our hotel room, a few feet from the edge of the water, he pushed me into the pool. No one had ever pushed me into a pool before. I had seen it in movies and TV shows where, after the initial surprise, they make out and their clothes cling in all the right places and their hair looks sexy wet. I was wearing the new red pleated skirt my mother bought me the last time I visited her in Chicago. The pleats would lose their crease, I was sure. After he pushed me, he jumped into the pool, too, and we splashed each other and laughed. Then, a few minutes later, as we got out, I became self-conscious and worried that my wet clothes stuck to my body in the wrong places. My hair looked stringy. I tried to play it off that I was carefree, that I was one of those kinds of girls that could just go with the flow, that it was no big deal that I was all wet and I didn't know where my sandals were. They fell off when he pushed me. I didn't realize until later that the night in the pool was a form of courting. The only way Khalil knew how to flirt with me was by pushing me in the pool like a child at a birthday pool party chasing the kid he likes.

Looking back now, though, it's clear there was more happening that night he shoved me into the pool than boyish flirting. Maybe Khalil's pushing me was a power move, as though this act somehow might alleviate the humiliation he felt that afternoon when he was searched by the Israeli soldiers. When we were in the car, I was more protected than he was—even as a young woman surrounded by the male soldiers, I had more power than Khalil. I even yielded some sort of sexual energy with the soldiers as I flirted with them. Perhaps pushing me in the pool was Khalil's way of acting out his upset from the afternoon.

We didn't have sex that weekend, but we did later in Jerusalem. We would spend many evenings in Jerusalem or around Ramallah—he'd drive me past his brother's house but never invite me in—and Bethlehem, trips to Tel-Aviv, his pointing out where olive groves used to be, his pride in having knowledge about his homeland and his desire to share this with an American Jew. "See those pine trees over there?" he'd point as we drove around. "Those were planted by the JUF. They used to be Palestinian villages." I wouldn't believe him until years later, even though I still have the certificate of planting a tree in Israel when I was seven with my allowance money. I was helping make the forest grow. Later, I'd read that pine trees aren't even native to the Middle East and were planted deliberately to cover up the Palestinian villages.

A youthful innocence hovered over us as we navigated our way around Palestinian and Israeli areas. We lived there but didn't live there. We believed the soil we walked on was our history, our home. And it was of course, in how we'd been taught, but we didn't really know what it was like to work there and pay taxes and to live there permanently. Khalil knew more than me, though, about life under occupation. And his family was from there. Mine wasn't. My great-grandparents were from Russia and Romania. But I was taught that a straight line existed between Israel and the beginning of the world—and the beginning of my life—and I could draw this line, and it was all mine. When I was there, I was told, I was home. But it wasn't true. We used this Middle Eastern temporary home as a playground, a getaway respite from our lives in the U.S. We spent our evenings driving around on hot summer nights, smoking cigarettes, our arms hanging out the windows touching the outside of the car door, moving our hands with the music that made it too loud to talk. A new radio station had just emerged, playing English, Arabic, and Hebrew music. We ashed our cigarettes out the window onto the landscape we both loved.

A couple months after the weekend in Eilat, Khalil was arrested and put in jail for a week as part of a group unsealing Palestinian homes sealed by Israeli soldiers. I knew he had become more active in the Palestinian community, but I didn't know much more than that. I went with some friends to visit him and his brother, a lawyer, explained to us that many Palestinians spend much of their time waiting at jails to see loved ones who are locked away. I wasn't a family member, so I couldn't see Khalil while he was in jail. And his brother didn't know we were spending so much time together, so I just told him to tell Khalil I said, "Hey."

The night he was released, he took a taxi from the jail to my apartment, took a shower, lay on the bed, and kissed me. He told me his stint in jail was a rite of passage for him, a Palestinian born in the U.S. who felt like he needed to prove himself in Palestine. He said he now had "legitimacy" in the Palestinian community because he was seen as resisting the occupation by getting arrested. "I have dinner invitations from half the town," he laughed. He got on top of me, then, this man torn between his Western and Eastern selves. As he kissed me, his gold necklace, the shape of Palestine, pointed into my neck as we moved our bodies together in the night, his first night out of jail, the point going in between my necklace, the bowed and swelled chai. He didn't stay over. In the middle of the night he got dressed, kissed my forehead, and drove back to Ramallah.

I have often wondered why, after gaining legitimacy among the Palestinian community, Khalil chose to come to a Jew's home in West Jerusalem the night he got out of jail. He might have said simply that the chance for sex was high. Or that, as an American, he still felt more comfortable in the Western part of the city. I romanticized my answer. I thought that perhaps there were complexities in that night interweaving and intersecting, beyond the sweat of our youth. Both of our identities, Khalil's and mine—I'd like to have believed—were as tangled and unraveled as the necklaces we both wore. But things weren't as complicated as I would have liked. We were both horny Americans in our twenties and we had both superimposed our best selves onto a landscape that was foreign, but one that we had also been told was our home.

A few months after we had been dating—and far too young to comprehend the political implications of a Shakespeare play being performed in Israel—I saw a poster for *Romeo and Juliet* being performed in Jerusalem at a theatre a ten-minute walk from my apartment. I anxiously bought two tickets, imagining Khalil's face when I would surprise him with the tickets. Although I wasn't sure how he would react to my asking him to see the play with me, I was confident that he would appreciate the metaphor of our being "star-crossed lovers," given we were a Palestinian and a Jew, navigating the Middle East together while our bedrooms in our homes in the U.S. remained empty and kept clean by our parents. I found out that the play was going to be a joint production with the Israeli Khan and the Palestinian El-Qasaba theaters.

The performance was held in an old hall used by the Israeli Electric Corporation behind the Jerusalem railway station. Juliet and the Capulets would be the Israelis and would speak Hebrew, while Romeo and the Montagues would be the Palestinians and would speak Arabic. English would be projected on a screen above the stage. I surprised Khalil with the tickets the next time he came over.

The play delivered. The street fight at the beginning of the play between the Montagues and Capulets was a metaphor for clashes between Israelis and Palestinians. The love between Romeo and Juliet—their speaking two different languages to each other—was romantic, especially given how difficult it was for them to be together. I wondered if any of the Israeli and Palestinian actors in real life were dating each other. I was particularly moved at the end when rocks—the symbol of the Intifada—were thrown onto the stage. It wasn't clear who had thrown them, for all of a sudden, they were thrown up onto the stage from the audience. How edgy, I thought, to be in

Jerusalem watching a Shakespeare play that acknowledges this symbol of Palestinian resistance.

When Romeo and Juliet, doomed lovers from the beginning of the play, kissed on the stage, an Israeli and a Palestinian, I looked next to me at Khalil, and was excited to fool around with him later. After the show, Khalil said he thought the play "was just okay." I assumed his lack of enthusiasm came more from his business background and general disinterest in the theatre than from his assumption that the Capulets and Montagues would be portrayed equally, "both alike in dignity," as the prologue tells us, ignoring the true power imbalance among Israelis and Palestinians. How could I have felt so good, I wondered years later, and not have seen the implications of performing such a play in Jerusalem, the real conflict between Israelis and Palestinians presented as one that was balanced and equal?

Others also had issues with the play, I learned. Freddie Rokem argues in his essay, "Postcard from the Peace Process," in the *Palestine-Israel Journal,* that the play does not address even basic power imbalances between Israelis and Palestinians. The performance in Jerusalem, Rokem writes, "merely reproduces the different hegemonic power structures as they have developed since 1967, as seen from an Israeli perspective." While the intentions of both directors were to "shock" the audience by performing a bilingual version of the play that people in Jerusalem hadn't seen before, it simply wasn't enough. "Political theater has to be dangerous and daring," Rokem writes. "And in order to be that, it is not enough to bring actors from the two peoples together and to present a bilingual performance." I wasn't aware of the politics that went into the production beyond knowing that there had been hassles for Palestinians to get through checkpoints for rehearsals in Jerusalem. I had taken for granted, as Rokem suggests, "all the other minor details in Jerusalem which in fact represent Israeli hegemony." I wasn't thinking of power dynamics and sub-narratives pitted against a dominant norm. I was thinking of Khalil and me and our tangled necklaces and the exaggerated love that I had projected onto our relationship and onto the stage. I had wanted our being together to be more than it was.

The evening that Khalil and I went to the play was our last. Afterwards, when he pulled up in front of my apartment, we sat in his car and he told me that he was going back to the U.S. for a while, "and when I come back here, I think we should just be friends." Naïvely, I thought that our seeing *Romeo and Juliet* would bring us closer, but it did the opposite. I understand now that the portrayal of the two families as equal was an insult to him; he just didn't have the language to explain it to me. Despite our both being from the U.S., things were not equal; we had no common world view. And we were too young—and politically unsophisticated—to understand.

Khalil didn't come back like he said he would. He attended graduate school in New York and now lives in Connecticut with his wife and kids. I found him on Facebook recently and told him I was writing this essay. I sent him a draft. Reading it brought back a lot of memories for him, he wrote. We were so young, he said in the letter, twice. He hasn't been back to Palestine, he wrote, because Israel won't let him in. When he wants to see his family, they all meet in Jordan. I remember the only letter he wrote me from the U.S. soon after we saw the play. On the envelope, he had written, "Jerusalem via Israel," a small gesture of political resistance. The Israel that invited Jews like me was the same nation-state that prevented his family from their true homeland, Palestine. We had used our respective homelands, Israel and Palestine, as a playground in the present tense. But it wasn't a playground for Khalil and his family, and he had had enough.

The day after the play, the day after Khalil broke up with me, I went back to the theatre and stole a poster which is framed, now, in my living room in Chicago. It's gold and blue and black with Arabic and Hebrew writing. The size of the letters in each language is exactly the same—equal at last—on a ripped poster sitting behind glass. The gold ribbon in the poster that wraps itself around Romeo and Juliet reminds me of the gold of our necklaces, bought in different jewelry stores in East and West Jerusalem. Average quality metal at best.

Was Dracula Jewish?

Last week, as I was prepping for my 11th grade English class, I reread the Greek creation myth where Rhea wraps a stone in swaddling clothes, pretending it's Zeus, whom she's hidden to protect him from his father Cronus. In the particular Greek myth I'll be using with students, the stone Rhea wraps is called an omphalos. In Greek, "omphalos" means navel, or the center of something. When I saw it last week, I realized I hadn't thought about the word since I was a graduate student in the 1990s at Hebrew University in Jerusalem studying literature. Both Jewish and Christian ancient religious texts consider Jerusalem the geographical and spiritual navel—or omphalos—of the earth. As early as the second century, Jerusalem was put at the center on cartographic images and called the "navel" of the earth.

A flurry of memories came rushing forward in my mind as I sat my lesson planning aside. Omphalos was also the name of the Hebrew University English Department's literary magazine that existed from 1993-2000. The founding editors called it *Omphalos* as a nod to this idea of Jerusalem as the navel of the world. And we, who ran the journal, gazed with bravado, a youthful superiority, from high up in the hills of the city, and even higher in the hills of Hebrew University, as we decided what pieces were deemed worthy of being published in *Omphalos*. I was a young Zionist fulfilling my birthright to live and study in Jerusalem, falling in love with the city and its stones and smells. The name of the journal was an homage, as well, to James Joyce—in one of Stephen Dedalus's stream of consciousness narrations, he says, "Will you be as gods? Gaze in your omphalos."

In 1994, I was on the editorial committee of *Omphalos* with other English Department students. Weekly, for several months, we would get together and look through submissions and decide whose pieces should go in that year's magazine. As an editorial team, we agreed on many pieces, most of which over-emphasized the soul, love, and God—seemingly fitting for young students studying literature in Jerusalem. Steve Talmai's poem, for example, played with the idea of roots and souls. Like most of us, he wrote poems of exaggerated cosmic self-importance. "They say I have lived / have roots growing out of my soul," he wrote in his poem, "Ghetto." I could relate. I was deeply in love with the city; the roots deep inside my soul had "come home" when I moved to Jerusalem.

At one of our first *Omphalos* meetings, we all agreed on a short prose piece by Uri Hershberg, "Before the First Word." It was a creation myth that pointed to modern problems: "before the Void could sap its resolve, the voice shouted at nothing in the middle of the uniform nowhere: Let there be light / and that's when the trouble started." We liked this piece—though maybe we'd cringe reading it now—because it felt edgy to us in the way it mocked the Bible; how risky to publish this in a literary journal in Jerusalem, we mused. We thought James Joyce would have been proud. Who were we to be as gods? We were gazing in our omphalos.

One day, when a new batch of submissions came in, I was particularly struck by a poem titled, "Was Dracula Jewish?" submitted anonymously by someone named X:

All I drink is wine

never see the sun shine

Sleep all day.

> My roommate is out studying Judaism
>
> and all that far out mysticism
>
> Trying to find a way.
>
> Till dawn I read the greats
>
> smoking too many cigarettes
>
> Just finished Hemingway.
>
> I get my second wind at two-ish
>
> wondering if Dracula was Jewish
>
> I'll wake up someday.

I was the only one on the editorial committee who liked it. The others thought X's poem was self-obsessive nonsense. I was outnumbered; X's poem was quickly tossed into the reject pile. For weeks I thought about the poem and its author. Who was X? Could I have known him? I had assumed, perhaps wrongly, that X was male. The only people I knew who read Hemingway in college were guys. Could I have walked by X on campus? Maybe he was an American Jew, like me, studying abroad. Or perhaps he had made aliyah, and had been living in Israel for a while now. I wondered what kind of mysticism X's roommate was studying and if he had in fact, as the poem suggested, succeeded in trying to find a way. I tried to think of reasons why X was drinking wine and sleeping all day. I wondered which Hemingway he was reading and if, as he indicated, he would wake up someday. Most of all, I thought about why X would wonder whether or not Dracula was Jewish.

X wasn't the first to question Dracula's potential Jewishness, of course. Many scholars have written about the Jewish—and anti-Semitic—characteristics in Bram Stoker's *Dracula*. In his book on the historical changes in the idea of the Gothic monster, *Skin Shows: Gothic Horror and the Technology of Monsters*, Jack Halberstam argues that "Gothic anti-Semitism portrays the Jew as monster." Stoker's *Dracula*, according to Halberstam, was a product of nineteenth-century European anti-Semitism. His Dracula was an ambiguous stereotypical Jew, who ultimately reflects "the Jew of anti-Semitism." *Dracula*, published in 1897, also coincided with the vast growth of Jewish emigration from Eastern Europe, and many scholars argue that the portrayal of Stoker's Dracula contributed to the "othering" of Jewish immigrants. "The monster Jew produced by nineteenth-century anti-Semitism represents fears about race, class, sexuality and empire," Halberstam maintains, and "this figure is indeed Gothicized or transformed into an all-purpose monster" in Dracula. I wondered why X had decided to write about a monster who he thought might be Jewish. Perhaps X felt like an outsider and identified with the vampire, who, as Halberstam argues in his book, "is otherness itself."

Stoker was not the first to link vampirism with Judaism. It is a stereotype that predates the wave of Jewish immigration that emerged from his novel. Sara Libby Robinson, in her book *Blood Will Tell: Vampires as Political Metaphors Before World War I* also discusses Bram Stoker's curious choice to give his Dracula distinctly stereotypical Jewish features like his hooked nose, pointed ears, and sharp teeth. Robinson argues that these Jewish stereotypes—which also included vampire metaphors, blood libel, and financial greed—existed decades before Stoker's book. Maybe X had read about these anti-Semitic Jewish stereotypes that Stoker's Dracula embodies when he wrote his poem. Perhaps X had experienced anti-Semitism in his life; maybe this contributed to his wanting to study in Israel. Or, perhaps like me, X had simply fallen in love with Jerusalem and liked writing about monsters as I had; both of us Zionists fulfilling our right to live in Israel.

I was sure our paths must have crossed. I guessed that X was an undergraduate because it seemed from his poem that he was discovering "the greats" for the first time. Had X been a graduate student, I think the poem might have indicated some already established awareness of the literary canon. He probably lived in the Resnick dorms on Churchill Boulevard, right across the street from the university. I lived in Idelson, on Lehi Street, the graduate dorm about a fifteen-minute walk from Resnick. I'm sure we both arrived in

Jerusalem in the summer to take ulpan, the intensive Hebrew immersion course required for all foreign students. Our morning hours would have been the same, then, since ulpan ran from 8:00 am-12:00 pm every day. He might have gathered, like I did each morning, in the Forum—the meeting place in the center of the campus—before ulpan started, to meet up with others and drink coffee. Then, at noon, the surge of students would fill the campus after ulpan ended. I'm sure I would have seen X then.

Despite my disappointment in X's poem not being chosen, we had a pretty good final product. The June 1994 issue of *Omphalos* had 35 poems and one short story. I didn't like any of them as much as X's poem, though. The editorial staff's favorite was Joy Bernstein's "Miracles." Her poem indicated that she was "waiting for God." Perhaps the rest of the editorial staff was waiting for God, too, in Jerusalem. X wasn't. He was wondering if Dracula was Jewish. And I was still upset that we never even discussed X's poem, which wasn't, as the others had suggested, self-indulgent nonsense to me.

Soon after the issue came out, I began to pull away from the editorial committee. I started hanging out in cafes by myself in downtown West Jerusalem, journaling who I imagined X to be. I began reading Hemingway as X indicated he did. Like X, I was smoking too many cigarettes; I even took cigarette breaks at *Omphalos* meetings and went outside to smoke, hoping that perhaps X would walk by—not thinking that I wouldn't know it if he did. I even tried to get a second wind at two-ish, like X, but failed most nights. As the weeks went by, my obsession with X deepened. He had no idea, of course, that I was piecing together a narrative of his life based on the poem he wrote. The few friends I had didn't know about my obsession either. It was much easier to fixate on X than to develop real relationships. As a result, I didn't return to the magazine the next year.

Though I continued to attend classes, I felt more detached from other Israeli students once I quit *Omphalos*. They were in their native country, whereas I was an American on a student visa. They served in the army and spoke perfect Hebrew, and most went home each weekend to their families in other cities across Israel. I remember one woman, Safa, though, with short black hair and thick arched eyebrows and swirly black eyeliner who sat next to me in our Shakespeare seminar. We had both been in the Toni Morrison and William Faulkner class the semester before, and she was nicer to me than the other Israeli women. When she'd arrive to class before me, she'd nonchalantly put her notebook in the seat next to her, saving the chair for me. When I noticed Arabic writing on the notebook as I sat down, I realized that Safa was Palestinian. I was embarrassed that I hadn't known. "What difference would it have made?" she'd ask me later once we became friends. But before we were close, and before I thought about the significance of Safa's identity, I mostly daydreamed about X.

    X and I would have really connected, I convinced myself. We would have hung out all the time. We would have sat in bars late at night in downtown West Jerusalem, like Champs, or Mike's Place, or the Underground Bar, and talked about Hemingway for sure, and Bukowski, and Carver. I was sure he would have come home with me one night to my apartment on Palmach Street in the Katamon neighborhood, and I'd have played him the audio cassette tape my ex-boyfriend Mark sent me from Chicago of Bukowski doing a reading while getting progressively more drunk with each poem. At one point towards the end of the reading, he falls off his stool in the middle of reading his poem, "The Wine of Forever." We would have smoked too many cigarettes, pontificating about the greats, thinking, at least, in the back of our minds, that we'd wake up someday. Maybe we could have felt alone, together—a phenomenon I find more realistic in my adult relationships now—as we gazed in and out of our respective omphalos.

    Later, I began to feel more like an outsider at the university. One afternoon months after I had quit *Omphalos,* Safa asked me in class if I was okay. I had been skipping our Samuel Beckett seminar and she was worried. Though I didn't tell her about my obsession with X, I did start spending more time with her. The first time was after class when she asked me if I wanted to have a coffee with her. "And a cigarette," she laughed, as she methodically rolled her own as the steam from the coffee reached her tongue that licked the rolling paper. I learned about her family in Nazareth, a Palestinian city a couple hours north of Jerusalem. "I'm a Palestinian citizen of Israel," she said. "My identity is different from Palestinians in the West Bank," she explained, "since I have an Israeli passport and they don't." Safa lived in the same dorm as I did, but with other Palestinian citizens of Israel, whereas I lived with Israeli Jews.

One day when she invited me to her dorm room for tea, I noticed she was melting wax in a pot on the stove next to the boiling tea. The wax was yellow and thick. She stirred it with a stick. She told me it was to remove the dark hair from her arms and that all the women in her family did this. The wax smelled like vanilla, or mint, or maybe it was the tea. I'm not sure now. She was embarrassed about how dark her hair was, she said, explaining she was much darker than Israeli women. I remember sitting that late afternoon in her room sipping tea, smoking her rolled cigarettes, the western sun coming in the small, square-shaped window where we blew out our cigarette smoke, watching her rip the hair off her arms with strips of wax. We'd become close, Safa and me, though we never talked about it. We had gravitated to each other naturally like awkward teenagers who don't fit in at a school dance.

As a result of starting to feel more on the margins socially, and beginning to understand some of the ways Safa, a Palestinian woman, felt marginalized systemically in Israeli society, I became more interested in Dracula's "otherness" too. I thought maybe I could stay connected to X—to my invention of him—if I learned more about Dracula. In his book, *Religion and its Monsters,* Timothy Beal explores Dracula's "monstrous otherness," and argues that Dracula is both an outsider and an insider. His home is "the East within the West, the Orient within the Occident." Dracula both fits in and doesn't fit in. I saw how this was true for Safa—my only real friend in Jerusalem—as well. I, too, could relate to Dracula's in-betweenness and I guessed that X also did. It seemed romantic to me that X lived beyond the mundane drudgery of the everyday. I imagined him up all night thinking about the greats while the rest of the city was sleeping, and like a hipster Dracula he would sleep all day when others were working. He was above it all, edgy, countercultural. He was beholden to no one—except, perhaps, his parents who were probably paying the bills for his stay in Jerusalem—yet he still longed to be a part of the world and show who he was by submitting his work for publication to *Omphalos.*

As I got to know Safa better, she told me other stories of her family, who has lived in Nazareth since the 1840s. In 1948, Nazareth fell under Israeli Zionist rule and has been occupied by Israel ever since. Aware of the significance of Nazareth's Christian history, Israel "spared"—she made quotation marks with her fingers as she said the word—the city's inhabitants the ethnic cleansing and expulsion that other Palestinians experienced. The city still suffers today, largely due to the Jewish Israeli settlement, Nazareth Illit, which has taken resources away from Nazareth and prevented the city from expanding, all while under Israel's occupation. Safa told me that though her family was educated, they didn't have the same access to education or jobs that Israelis do. Their neighborhoods' roads and resources are much lower quality than Israeli neighborhoods. She was the first one in her family, she told me, to attend Hebrew University. And she was really excited—I'd realize the irony later—to read Hemingway for the first time next semester.

As my friendship deepened with Safa, I began to think differently about Zionism. I was taught from an early age that the Jews came to settle the land and make the desert bloom. "A land without a people for a people without a land," I learned at Zionist summer camp, where, along with other mostly upper middle-class suburban Jews, we exhibited a kind of liberalism that never involved talking about Palestine. When I think about it now, I realize a significant flaw in the mythology I was taught. If the land was empty, as I was told, who were the Palestinians in the photos I've seen who "left" the land—ethnically cleansed and expelled, I would learn later—in 1948 with everything they could carry on their backs; where did they come from if the land was empty? And who were the Arabs who fought in 1948? I think I remember asking adults these questions as a child—I was starting to notice a hole in the logic—and being told by teachers at Hebrew school that the land was empty and, at the same time, that the land had been inhabited by Palestinians who, in 1948, willingly left on their own. Those who fought, my teachers told me, came from neighboring Arab countries, none of which wanted Israel to become a state.

This logistical impossibility doesn't make sense; but myths don't have to. Myths don't rely on reason or logic. Cronus eats his children, one by one, except for Zeus, whom Rhea hides. When Cronus disgorges his children and the omphalos, the children come out all grown up. Myths don't have to make sense. They perpetuate a narrative. The myth that Israel is a democracy, a just society founded on righteousness and goodness pulls at the heartstrings of Zionists everywhere, while the reality of Israel as an occupying nation denying indigenous Palestinians the dignity to a self-determined existence remains hidden inside the myth for those who want to believe it. Safa's story was different from the stories I was told. The land wasn't vacant, awaiting the Jews to settle it, and it challenged what I was taught by those I loved and trusted the most. Every single Palestinian I have met since Safa has told me similar stories and they have all been antithetical to the narrative with which I was raised.

Looking back now, I realize my questioning Zionism had further distanced me from the *Omphalos* editorial committee—though I wasn't aware at the time—all of whom were ardent Zionists and only spent time with other Jews. I didn't yet understand that before 1948, Palestinians had lived in all areas of Jerusalem, not just the East, and in Jaffa, and Tel-Aviv, and in all the cities and villages that dot the landscape. But as I look back now, Safa was my first entry into a narrative different from the Zionist narrative I was taught. My anti-Zionism would come later, in stages, and would further separate me from loved ones as I, too, became marginalized for thinking differently.

Once I began spending time in East Jerusalem—on and around Salah Al-Din and St. George Streets—I learned more about the Palestinians who lived there. They were not the monsters I was told about. As my interest in the Palestinian narrative grew, I felt even more marginalized among Jews. None of the Jewish friends I used to have would ever have gone to East Jerusalem with me. A couple years later, after I'd given up on X, I'd try my luck with an actual real human, and would fall in love with Tavit, who worked in his father's shop in East Jerusalem. He would take me to different parts of Ramallah and Bethlehem and Hebron than Khalil showed me and then would buy me drinks in the same bars I'd imagined I might have gone with X in West Jerusalem. Like Khalil, Safa, and me, Tavit fit in and didn't fit in. A member of the Armenian minority, he zigzagged seamlessly between East and West Jerusalem, using his Arabic or Hebrew or Armenian or English depending on his location.

While Safa was a real systemic representation of otherness, as a Palestinian within Israel, X remained my quiet obsessive made-up marginalized character. I wondered if the Dracula X portrayed in his poem could have lacked national pride, a "lack of an allegiance to a fatherland," as Halberstam writes in her book. Perhaps X questioned his national loyalty to Israel like me, a Jew stuck in the melodramatic dark night of the diaspora. Mordecai, the Jewish character in George Eliot's 1876 novel, *Daniel Deronda,* for example, whom Robinson also discusses in her book, is an ardent Zionist devoted to creating a Jewish homeland in Palestine. Mordecai equates vampirism with a lack of patriotism. "The inhabitant of any country must pledge his loyalty, his energy, his blood, with the interests of his fellow citizens," Mordecai insists. "Anything that detracts from these vows of kinship cannot help but turn an individual into a parasite of their country's resources and goodwill—in other words, a vampire." I remember writing my undergraduate thesis on *Daniel Deronda* in 1992, a year before I'd move to Jerusalem, exploring the ways in which Eliot's novel was a Zionist call for Jews like Mordecai—and me—to return to Palestine.

Once I was back in Chicago many years later, though, long after I had left Jerusalem, in a graduate seminar on post-colonialism—I got a second master's degree—when I read Edward Said's "Zionism From the Standpoint of Its Victims," more than once and I would learn, ultimately abandoning the Zionism with which I was raised, that Eliot associates Zionism with civilized, Western thought and that Jews like Mordecai believed he would bring this Western civility to Palestine in the East, which he considered savage and barbaric. Eliot believes, according to Said, that the bridge between the East and the West "will be Zionism." After reading Said, I realized my thesis—all born of my love for Israel and literature and Zionism—was useless.

I wondered if X would ever come to see Zionism from the standpoint of its victims, like I was beginning to. Maybe, like me, after some time, he left the hills of Hebrew University—perhaps, briefly, stopped gazing in his omphalos. Before I left, though, and in spite of not returning to *Omphalos,* I submitted a short story the following year. Despite having distanced myself so much, the editors accepted my piece. The exaggerated cosmic self-importance—I wince reading it now—saturated this issue as well. My story, untitled, began, "In an attempt to preserve her immortal thoughts, she vigorously inscribed her words as the innocence slowly leaked from her soul." Like the other pieces, mine was full of relationship drama peppered with Biblical references. But it was true. My innocence of the Zionist narrative had slowly leaked from my soul—cringe-worthy phrasing aside. I just didn't know it then. I hoped that X might have read my piece. Maybe he would have wondered who I was—though unlike him, my name was listed, so he actually could have found me quite easily. By the time the *Omphalos* issue came out, Safa had moved back to Nazareth with her family for the summer. I soon fell in love with Tavit and eventually finished my master's degree. Safa went on to get her Ph.D. in Literature, and now chairs the English Department at a small college near Nazareth.

I remained the only one who ever liked X's poem and I never learned anything about him. I never told anyone about him either, except my husband (and I think also, perhaps, my mother, decades ago in a letter) who recently saw X's poem sitting on my desk while I've been writing this essay and asked me about the crumpled paper from 1993. In childlike terms, my creation of X showed me that I could be on the margins and still be okay. But it was a youthful folly, high up on a hill. And I am sure, after all that I conjured, X's poem was likely more of a drunken scribble one night in a dorm than the myth I had created of him. At the time, it was much easier to obsess on men who wrote anonymous poems than to deal with the paradigm shifts occurring within me. I had discovered that the real monsters were the ones I had trusted who had told me about other monsters who weren't monsters. But I was still in love with Jerusalem and I didn't know what to do with these feelings.

X had served a purpose for me in Jerusalem—perhaps nothing more than a distraction from myself, for I had projected onto him what others would come to see as monstrous and marginalized in me as I became more anti-Zionist—and I'd miss him, and Safa, like I do even now, planning my curriculum lessons on Greek myths for high school students in Chicago. There was no Rhea to swaddle me in Jerusalem. Left to my own obsessions with monsters and Zionism, I fit inside of nowhere but the real and made up stories of lovers and others. I never discussed Hemingway with either of them. Who are any of us, after all, in our youth, to say we are not monstrous? Or to claim that we ever fit in, trying to find a way? Who do we think we are, really, to believe a myth and gaze into our omphalos day after day and to assert to anyone that someday we'll wake up.

A Meandering, Sometimes Agonizing Path

"Do you have kids?" Aviva asked, dipping her bread into the soup at our lunch in Jerusalem.

It made sense, I suppose, that she would want to know. We hadn't seen each other in 25 years, and women just seem to ask each other these things. It's an innocent, perhaps, nonchalant inquiry, I guess, because you either have them or you don't. But the question always strikes me as odd— one of those moments when something private suddenly becomes uncomfortably public.

Mismatched teal and orange chairs accompanied the square pale wood tables at the vegan restaurant where we had agreed to meet. I got there before Aviva who was running a few minutes late—she texted because she had to take a bus, then the Jerusalem tram that rolls down Jaffa Road, and was running behind schedule. Aviva and I met at Hebrew University in 1992. We were the same age, both earning our Master's Degrees in English Literature. Now it was winter, 2018, and I had a couple weeks off from the high school where I was teaching English. I hadn't been back to Israel in a few years, my husband and I had recently separated, I wanted to get far away from Chicago, so I thought it was a good time for a visit.

While I waited for Aviva, I watched two men next to me. They sat near an old space heater with metal coils hot and red that enabled their pita bread to stay warm. Two extension cords—a fire hazard, to be sure—made it possible for the heater to be in the middle of the restaurant. The two guys would break off a piece, scoop up some hummus, and put the rest of the bread back on the heater until their next bite.

Earlier, on my way to our lunch, I meandered around Jerusalem, on old, twisty, cobblestone roads, down Ben Yehuda and Yoel Solomon Streets, past galleries and cafes, to the vegan restaurant Aviva suggested near Kikar Tzion (Zion Square) just off Jaffa Road. I was a bit disoriented. Jerusalem had changed. East Jerusalem was more seamlessly connected to West Jerusalem—a strategic move on Israel's part, I was convinced. Upscale jewelry stores and baby clothes boutiques had replaced old dingy bars where expats used to hang out. New limestone construction stood next to older stone buildings, trying to emulate that both had always been there. Of course, I had changed, too. I had come far to get away from my current life in Chicago, but being back in Jerusalem also made me remember things from long ago as I walked on the cobblestones of the city.

The restaurant is on the original location of Champs, the pub I frequented in the evenings after my graduate seminars when I lived in Jerusalem in my 20s. I drank too many White Russians there—a cocktail made of vodka, coffee liqueur, and cream. "It tastes like Bailey's!" I used to joke with the guys I met there. This was the bar with the bartender, Israel. It was impossible to see any remaining clue that the hipster-grungy vegan restaurant where I was meeting Aviva was once the site of the bar—the only thing it had retained was its square structural shape and a few ghosts.

While I waited, I watched the two men eat their hummus and warm their pita on the space heater with the metal coils. When Aviva arrived, she looked very much like she did when we were in our 20s, a bohemian from Greenwich Village—stylish, urban, thin. She wore a brown corduroy skirt with zig-zagged patches, a black turtleneck sweater and dark brown ankle boots with light brown laces. The only difference I noticed, besides some aging in both of our faces, was the funky green hat she wore to cover her hair, the customary tradition in Orthodox Judaism indicating a woman is married. She was living in Ramot, the mostly Orthodox Jewish settlement about seven miles outside Jerusalem. She called the West Bank "Judea and Samaria," a nod to the Biblical reference that the land belongs to the Jews. She said the settlement isn't really a settlement, but more like a suburb of Jerusalem. "It's our land, anyway," she told me at lunch that day, like she had told me decades earlier. "God promised it to us."

Aviva had always been Orthodox. She knew who she was and what she wanted. My life has been much different. While I have a very strong Jewish identity, I am mostly secular, had married a Buddhist, and was newly separated. I was also Zionist and had dreamed of studying in Israel someday. Later, I would abandon the ideology we shared and would become more disillusioned by Israel's policies. When we were in grad school, Aviva lived on a famous street in Jerusalem, Sheshet HaYamim, (Six Days), a road named for the 1967 Six-Day War between Israel and its neighboring Arab countries. Like most of the street names in Jerusalem, this one represented a crucial turn in Israel's history, the war in which Israel occupied the Gaza Strip, West Bank, Golan Heights, and East Jerusalem—a Zionist nod to winning the war. Sheshet HaYamim was a beautiful street lined with limestone homes and big trees between the French Hill and Ramat Eshkol neighborhoods. It was her father's house, a prominent Rabbi who split his time between Jerusalem and their other home in Manhattan. Floor-to-ceiling bookshelves filled with Jewish texts crowded every room. In the dining room, a chunky, long wooden table where the family held its Shabbat dinners took up most of the space.

The first class Aviva and I were in together at Hebrew University in 1992 was our William Faulkner/Toni Morrison course. Aviva was petite, unassuming, and outspoken in all the classes we took together. We would talk for hours about how we preferred Shakespeare's tragedies to his comedies—*The Merchant of Venice*, *Romeo and Juliet*, *King Lear*, our favorites. In our Critical Literary Theory class we agreed with Hegel's insistence that art must serve man's inner life for it to be meaningful and with Kant's claim that poetry is the freest and highest form of art. "I admire that Hurston didn't want to have children," she said once in our Zora Neale Hurston class after reading *Their*

Eyes Were Watching God, "because she knew it would take her away from her writing and other things she wanted to accomplish in her life."

At lunch that day in Jerusalem, we ate hummus, and also tofu curry and sweet potato soup and, in addition to the pita, the homemade thick multi-grain bread that dripped and thickened as we dipped it in the soup—the bread she was eating when she asked me if I had kids. Aviva said she'd been thinking about getting back to painting, something she used to do before she got married. She was teaching English part-time at a few colleges in the area, and then she laughed, saying, "What else would either of us have done with our English degrees than teach?" When she told me she had six kids, I almost gagged on the multi-grain bread I was chewing. "You know us Orthodox always have a ton of children," she laughed, and then said, "But wait, get this." I waited. "Two of them voted for Trump," she said, as though she knew how outrageous it sounded. It wasn't all that strange, though, we both knew, given that she lived in Ramot. Many Orthodox Jews in Israel voted for Trump in 2016.

The two men who had been warming their pita on the heater had left.

Before I answered Aviva's question, I thought about the hysterectomy I had on November 8, 2016. The only reason I was grateful the surgery was on Election Day was the drugs I got for the pain. On the way back from the hospital, the anesthesia not yet worn off, Hillary signs everywhere passed me in a blur. Later that night, once home and on the couch in a semi-comfortable position, my husband and I watched the polls as it became clearer Trump would win. "Can I have one of your Vicodin," he asked me, "this is looking bad." In the morning, we were both in a fog, and I could barely walk. I watched the clock in four-hour increments with anticipation for when I could have another pill. It remained unclear to me whether my pain was coming more from my physical discomfort or the ominous feeling of what was to come after the election. Likely, it was both—the privacy of the hysterectomy had coincided with the most public of national events.

Several fibroids had grown in the walls of my uterus and needed to be removed. "They're the size of oranges, not quite cantaloupes," the doctor told me months before the surgery, "but give it time and they will be." I was 46 at the time and had decided years before not to have children, so the hysterectomy, while scary, wasn't devastating. Even so, I felt a twinge deep inside, an internal pinch, when the nurse explained why I had to give a urine sample the morning of the surgery. "Just in case you're pregnant," she said. My physical body was about to experience a finality with something my emotions had accepted years before, my organs catching up with my mind.

My reasons for not having kids are far less interesting to me today at 50 than they were at 40. Ten years ago I would have admitted that I was grieving the loss, that I had missed out on a crucial rite of passage known to the majority of women, that I think I would have parented well, or I'd wonder what kind of kid I might have had, the friends I might have made with other parents, whether I'd adopt if I couldn't have my own. But once I hit 44, the window about closed, it just didn't really matter anymore. I had simply filled my life with other things. When Aviva asked me that day at lunch if I had kids, it had been three years since my surgery and I really hadn't thought about it much. "But maybe your child would have been his generation's Moses or Gandhi," a Rabbi friend once said to me, in defense of having kids during difficult times. When I was young I thought I would have several like my mother did. "You need to have three," she once told me, "so at least one will help you when you're old."

Now that I'm older—and wondering, at times, who will care for me down the road, especially if my husband and I don't reconcile—I don't feel the need to apologize for not having kids like I used to or to provide a defensive retort of why it's okay not to. Mine isn't a unique story. I just didn't have them. I suppose one could argue that I lacked intention when I was younger, that I didn't put myself in situations where I'd meet someone I'd want to marry until I was 38 when I met my husband—unlike Aviva, who was dating furiously in her early 20s, determined to get married and have kids. I did, however, feel enormous pressure to have children when I was younger—or to *want* to have children. The rhetoric was drilled into me even more by having a father who was also a pediatrician, the penultimate in a child-rearing profession. (I did confess once, though, to a friend who also doesn't have kids that I was curious what it would have felt like to be pregnant. "I've thought about that, too," she admitted, "but I think you could emulate that feeling with drugs.") I was nonetheless relieved when I realized other women were out there without kids who had felt pressure, too. Most women "are goaded into thinking about it practically from birth," Meghan Daum writes in *Selfish, Shallow, and Self-Absorbed: Sixteen Writers on the Decision Not to Have Kids*. "Those of us who choose not to become parents are a bit like Unitarians or Californians," she confesses, "we tend to arrive at our destination via our own meandering, sometimes agonizing paths."

    While the fits and starts of my life that led me not to have children were, at times, agonizing, it often seemed more tragic to others than to me. Parents I knew looked at me strangely. "What exactly do you do on the weekends?" a colleague at the high school I teach at asked me once after questioning if I had children. "Do you have kids?" another asked me directly when I was new to the school. Before I could answer, she said with a wide, almost feverish smile, "No judgment if you don't!" At age 40, two weeks after I got married, another colleague cornered me in the school hallway, looking worried. It was 8:05 am, just a few minutes before first period began—I was about to begin teaching *Othello*—and she asked frantically what I was going to do about kids now that I had "gotten married so late." At age 46, a neighbor my age with a wife and two sons who lived, as I did, in a third-floor apartment, asked me on a Saturday night when I was sitting on my deck reading why I wasn't out dancing at the clubs. I told him I was tired and getting old, like him.

    "No," I answered Aviva. "I don't have kids." Though she was simply asking about my life, I felt that the question of children so often opens a woman's private life for public inspection. A waitress came to clear our plates. Outside the clouds were becoming gray. It was almost late-afternoon. It looked like it might rain. We had been sitting for a couple hours and the time had gone by fast.

"Sometimes I think I'd give up a couple kids to have created a couple good paintings," she joked, tossing her head back laughing. I got a glimpse of her light brown hair under her green hat.

"What's your husband like?" I asked.

"Well," she said, "let's just say I married him for the end." I must have looked like I didn't understand.

"I mean, we're not that close now, but he's the guy who will take me to the hospital at the end of my life when I'm dying. I married him for that. For the end. And, of course, for the children. He'll be the one to take me when I need chemo."

"Do you have cancer?" I asked.

"Not yet," she said.

Aviva's mother had died of breast cancer a couple years before we met. She died on Shabbat. Aviva was in the house on Sheshet HaYamim Street with her entire family after just being with their mother—she has six siblings—who was nearby at Hadassah Hospital. Since her family didn't use the phone on the Sabbath, the hospital agreed to call when her mother died. The signal would be two rings, then they'd drop the call, and then they'd call back and let the phone ring just once. That's how the family would know she died. "I named my fifth child after her," Aviva said.

One night in 1994 Aviva and I sat up late in her bed. She had invited me for Shabbat dinner with her family. After a loud evening of singing Hebrew songs and eating lemon chicken and talking about big and small things, we went upstairs. She wanted to show me a piece of paper she called her "dating list." The list had four columns: the name of the guy she had the date with, where they met, how long the date was, and how it went. "I'm up to 24," she told me. Then she leaned over to me in her bed and confessed how sexy she thought it was that Orthodox wives covered their hair in public. She described it as something private and sacred, and when she said she thought it was sexy, I thought it was sexy, too. I imagined Aviva, a virgin at the time, on top of her future husband, slowly taking off some stylish hat (funky green?), her long, light brown hair falling onto his face as she moved.

Orthodox Judaism—indeed, Aviva's predictable path—was so far removed from my life in Jerusalem it had become exotic to me. At the same time, because Aviva knew she was on a single trajectory to get married to an Orthodox man and have kids, my life of drinking in bars with non-Jewish men who didn't commit seemed foreign to her. I had recently fallen deeply in love with Tavit, a man I met at the pub and knew I'd never marry. We dated for two years, right up until the night I left Jerusalem for Chicago after finishing my studies. Looking back now, it seems unlikely that Tavit and I would have dated or that Aviva and I even became friends. Literature had bonded Aviva and I, though it had also made us different, too, for it was there, in fiction, where Aviva could experience alternative life-styles and ambiguity, whereas I had tried to emulate it in real-life.

I didn't stay over Shabbat evening at Aviva's because I was meeting Tavit later, where I'd hang out at a bar in East Jerusalem with his Armenian and Palestinian friends in a neighborhood in Jerusalem that wasn't Jewish at all, where no one observed Shabbat. Walking down Sheshet HaYamim street to meet him later that night, the quiet and dark seemed to emanate a sense of privacy as though out of respect for Shabbat. As I walked on the limestone sidewalk, I wondered what it might feel like to be Orthodox, to be part of a tight community, to not stray from the norm, to have only my husband see my hair. Once in a while I heard people handling dishes—the sounds of families who had shared a meal together. I made my way down to the Old City, through the Jaffa Gate into the Jewish Quarter, to the Armenian Quarter to meet Tavit at the crowded, loud bar. There, I wondered what it might have been like to be Armenian and be with Tavit as his Armenian wife and be part of another tight community, though I knew that would never happen. Instead, I stood on the stone street alone for just a moment before entering, one foot in each world. The reality, of course, was that I belonged to neither. I knew I'd return to Chicago after completing my master's degree, say goodbye to Tavit and Aviva, but after living abroad for several years, I'd have trouble fitting in anywhere once I returned.

Outside the vegan restaurant, it had become cloudy. In the winter, Jerusalem is wet and windy. It was time to go. When we left, an old Orthodox man rode past us on his bike with a shower cap covering his fedora hat. Rain must have been in the forecast, Aviva observed, as the man went by. I told her I'd walk her back to the tram on Jaffa Road.

All of a sudden, as we stood on the corner of Jaffa Road and Agrippas Street, about to say goodbye, Aviva said enthusiastically, "Oh, I forgot to tell you my idea for a short story."

I wanted to hear it. It would delay us a few minutes. I was feeling sad about leaving her. The tram stopped near where we were standing. "I'll get the next one," Aviva said. An Orthodox couple searched for their tickets before boarding the train. An old Arab man carrying three plastic bags of food walked by. Aviva began to tell me her idea.

"The story is about an Orthodox woman, a painter, who is preparing for her gallery opening. It's her first. She's gotten a cool space in an art gallery on King David Street, just over there around the corner." She pointed behind her towards the expensively-posh street.

"Right there, in the middle of downtown. Well, the Orthodox woman has six kids, see, and her painting life has been stifled for the last fifteen years. But with four of the kids older now, she's been dabbling a bit when her husband is at work. It's small canvases at first, and then, in their spare room downstairs, she's started to paint on larger ones."

"What kinds of things does she paint?" I asked her.

"Well, that's the thing," she said. Her voice lowered a bit. She leaned in closer towards me.

"Do you know what a bedikah is?" she asked. I didn't.

"A bedikah is what an Orthodox woman does to check if she still has her period. You know Hebrew, Liz, the word bedikah comes from the verb 'to check.' Well, when the woman thinks her period is ending, she takes a bedikah cloth, wraps it around her finger, and sticks it up there to check if there is any blood. If there isn't, then she can have sex with her husband again, since she's considered clean. But if the cloth has some blood on it, she has to do it again every day until there's nothing on it."

"You mean she has to finger herself?" I asked.

"Basically, yes," Aviva said, smiling.

A few weeks after my hysterectomy, I began pelvic floor physical therapy to strengthen the muscles that had become weak as a result of the surgery. My physical therapist, Sarah, a 40-year old woman who liked to tell me about her online dating experiences—"Most of the guys are such losers"—taught me to use a therawand, a plastic device that looks remarkably like a sex toy. It's used internally to loosen tight muscles in the pelvic floor.

"Where do you buy the cloths to do the bedikah?" I asked Aviva.

"Oh, that's easy," she answered, "you can order them on Amazon."

Another tram ambled down Jaffa Road. It started to drizzle. Aviva opened her umbrella and we both stood under it.

"Let me get back to my short story idea," she said, "because you're probably wondering what bedika has to do with painting." My right shoulder started to get wet; we didn't both fit fully under the umbrella.

"So the woman has been painting for a while in this spare room, see, and she gets this wild idea. She wants to paint canvases of bedikah cloths. Like what the cloth looks like when you pull your finger out and open the material and see if there is blood. Every time you do it, it looks different, like the way you wrap it around your finger, the shade of the pink or red blood, the folds of the cloth. Large, huge canvases she wants to paint. She starts with a couple small canvases and paints these rose-colored swirls, the way it looks when you take your finger out and open the cloth.

"But then she gets so into it that she buys all these bright colors of paint—orange, turquoise, yellow, tons of different greens and blues, purples and pinks, and starts painting on large canvases, using different sized paint brushes so she can really focus on accurately painting the folds of the bedikah cloth when it's wrapped around the finger. After a few months she has about twenty of these canvases, all different colors, all symbolic expressions of the bedikah—one of the most private acts for a woman.

"She hasn't told anyone. One evening in particular, when it's the time of the month for her to do the bedikah check, she props one foot on the toilet, her husband asleep in their bedroom nearby, and she pulls out the cloth. It's a light pink, and she's sure she's made that color pink before on her palette downstairs in the spare room.

"Well, one day, she's walking in downtown Jerusalem on King David Street, you know where all those art galleries are. She goes into one of them, a small storefront, and recognizes the owner from a mom's group she was in when her oldest was born. It'd been about twenty years since they had seen each other. They're talking about their kids, of course, and then she asks the gallery owner—she can't believe it just comes out so easily—if she might display her art. She describes it only as abstract images, not a representation of the bedikah, and pulls out some photos of a few paintings on her phone and shows the woman, who says she loves the colors and that they seem to be linked thematically, though in an abstract way.

"Another month goes by. It's the night of the art opening. She's got about eighteen paintings displayed in the space. She's told her friends and family about the art exhibit but she hasn't said specifically that they're paintings of the bedikah cloths. Her husband brings their kids. An hour before the exhibit, she wrapped a white bedikah cloth around her finger and did the manual check, fingering herself. The cloth was white. She was clean.

"The woman had spent weeks preparing for the exhibit, making decisions like which colors should be next to each other, how high each painting should be hung, where the light should hit each painting. On opening night, she wore a gray dress with black boots, wanting to be sure her outfit didn't take away from the bright colors of the paintings that hung all over the room. She didn't wear earrings. Her green hat was tilted just a bit.

"People began coming into the gallery, walking around. It didn't seem like anyone knew what the paintings were of, but they appreciated the abstract shapes and colors. When her husband showed up with the kids, she could tell he was proud of her. She watched him closely as he moved around the room, one eye on the kids and one on the paintings. Then, about a half hour later, she's pretty sure she caught his eye right at the moment when he figured out what she had painted. He looked at one painting, then another, then looked back, and all of a sudden she could see something click in his mind. He made the connection. He looked at her, and she at him, and she stood still, waiting to see his reaction.

"She had made a private ritual public," Aviva told me, her eyes widening as another tram went by. "She had taken one of the most intimate rituals that exists within the Orthodox community and splayed it on the wall for everyone to see. Her husband was surrounded by a rainbow of cloths that represented a woman's private life, walls of them, all different sizes, staring at him, saying, among many things, that the cloths had developed a kind of intimacy with his wife. All this went on as his wife without earrings in a gray dress watched him.

Once again, Aviva and I diverged: she relished bringing something personal and private into the public, whereas I preferred more privacy about my personal choices.

"Isn't that a crazy story?" she said, laughing. We were soaked from the rain.

"But then what happened?" I asked.

"I don't know," she shrugged her shoulders. "That's all I have."

"What do you mean?" I asked. "What does the husband do?"

"I don't know," she repeated. "I haven't figured that out."

Aviva checked her watch. "I've got to go, I'm late!" she announced, and kissed me on the cheek. "By the way," she whispered privately, winking as she was about to board the tram, "that story isn't about me." She waved to me as the doors shut in front of her.

I watched her walk towards a seat on the tram, watched the tram as it moved her back to the West Bank, back to Ramot, back to the husband she had married for the end. Aviva, who couldn't figure out an ending for the fictional story, was sure of the ending of her real-life one. I was annoyed and also fascinated by the lack of finality in her story and even more disturbed by the certainty of her real one. In a few days I'd return to Chicago, unsure of what my ending would be, wondering if perhaps the difference between a fictional and real story didn't even matter after all, all the private moments that make up a trajectory of a life. I tried not to think about it.

16-Year Old Love Story:
Once I Was Lit by Moonbeams

A couple of weeks ago a student of mine returned from spending the Passover holiday with his family in Israel. He's American, short and stocky with red hair. His older brother and sister are currently serving in the Israeli army. When I asked him what they did for Passover, he said they went "glamping," the term for "glamorous camping." Apparently, his family's version of glamping meant staying at the famous, and expensive, King David Hotel in Jerusalem. His week in Israel also included, he told me, visiting The Alexander Muss High School in Israel (AMHSI), which he'll be attending next year, for "an eight week academic experience," as described on the website. AMHSI is a high school program based in Hod Hasharon, a small town 25 minutes outside Tel-Aviv, founded in 1972 by Rabbi Morris Kipper and the Miami Jewish Federation. Part of its mission, the Jewish Federation website says, is for "students [to] visit all parts of the country for first-hand experiences and learning, helping to create a lifelong love and attachment to the Jewish homeland."

I attended AMHSI in 1986 when I was 16 years old—my first trip to Israel—during the summer in between 11th and 12th grade. Max, a friend of mine from the Zionist-Socialist Jewish camp we attended, Habonim, persuaded me to attend the program. "It's like camp," he said, "but in Israel." It seemed a natural progression to go from the Jewish camp that simulated living in Israel to the real thing. After years of nationalist foreplay at the camp in Michigan, I'd finally consummate my love by setting foot on the land. I sold the trip to my father by emphasizing the "academic experience" part of the eight-week program. We'd study in the mornings, I explained to him, and then visit the places we learned about in the afternoons. I could even get high school credit, I told him.

Although I knew we weren't poor, I also knew we weren't swimming in money. But all the years of sending me to the Jewish camp had been expensive. Both of my parents grew up working class, and though they were thriving in successful careers, they had to spend and save wisely. Their relationship to money was very different from many of their friends and mine who had tons of it and spent indiscriminately.

My father agreed to send me to Israel if I got a job to help cover the spending money I'd need. I found work at Kosher City, the local kosher deli down the street from our house. On Sundays from March until the week I left for Israel in June, I cut heads off fish, weighed cheese, and sliced meats. I was paid $3.75 an hour under the table. I made a few hundred dollars, but my father led me to believe that my work significantly helped fund my first trip to Israel. I would be out of my league financially, though, once I arrived and met the others. I had brought $300 as my spending money—the equivalent is about $700 today—to last the eight weeks, whereas others' parents wired that much every week, most of which was spent on alcohol. Girls in the dorm laughed at my worn suitcase bought at JCPenney, borrowed from my father, as theirs showed off new monograms and shiny colors by designers I didn't know.

At the school, I was the nerd who loved the coursework. Others blew it off and were excited that Israel didn't have a drinking age. I took copious notes in the different booklets we were given. In the classroom we were often put into groups with special names that represented different parts of Israel: Galil, Golan, Judea, Samaria, Kineret, and Shomron. I was in the Golan group. Aaron, from Boston, with long, black hair and round wire glasses, whom I soon developed a crush on, was in Galil. The curriculum had eight units: Biblical Period; Bayit Sheni (Second Temple) and Talmudic Periods; The Middle Ages; Emancipation, Haskala and Zionism; The State on its Way: 1914-1947; Hasho'a (The Holocaust); Medinat Yisrael (The State of Israel); and The Appendix.

I wrote my name on the top of each booklet—often inside of a heart I drew around it—and marveled at all of the resources in each one. I believed the curriculum to be truth; after all, each booklet was full of primary documents that backed up everything we learned. The teachers, Yoav and Jonah, constantly supported the claims they made, all justifying Jews' right to the land of Israel, with evidence from the texts.

In Unit 4: Emancipation, Haskala and Zionism, we read a selection by Margalit Ornstein under the heading "Cultural Zionism." Ornstein, considered the "founding mother" of Israeli dance, immigrated to Palestine—the word Palestine was used only in reference to pre-1948 Israel—in 1921 from Austria, wrote:

> On the flat roof among the many and mighty Judean mountains, lit by the moon beams and covered by the rich suede cloak of dusk—a man and a woman express in dance their heart's desire; through their movements they express the eternal truth which cannot be uttered in words. And here a large flower garden, shining and glorifying in majesty and variety of colors. It is full of children, many beautiful children, with solid and flexible bodies. Their skin is a golden velvet from the sun's kisses, made gentle by the wind and pure air. They dance and sing with a happy and free rhythm. Behold our liberated and renewed nation in its dance.

We youngsters from the diaspora, too, had solid and flexible bodies. We, too, gazed at the Judean mountains lit by the moon beams. Having arrived in Israel, we also moved differently, as do the children of Israel in Ornstein's passage. Her words—terribly Orientalist and colonialist to me now—made us feel deeply connected to the land even pre-1948, "which means it's undeniably ours," our teacher Yoav said. But this was one passage in one booklet out of the eight booklets that had thousands of passages just like this one. We were sold.

Soon after reading this section on Cultural Zionism, we made our way at night to Tel-Aviv, dancing at the Dolphinarium—later bombed in 2001—drinking and moving our bodies like the free Zionist spirits we had read about earlier. I was much more comfortable studying in the classroom and visiting the "ancient and historic sites"—all indigenous Palestine, I would realize later—than dancing at a nightclub. I went to follow the crowd, though, and also because Aaron (from the Galil group) went too. Soon, however, we both found ourselves outside, frustrated that the others only came to Israel, it seemed, to party and hook up. I would do those things later on subsequent trips to Israel, but that particular summer, my first time there, a virgin in Israel, I was very serious about learning all I could. Years later when I was ready for relationships, I'd discover I was at a disadvantage. I'd have no idea how to make real connections with flawed human beings, for I'd fallen in love with an ideal. The idealized Israel I'd been in love with for so many years, the one presented to me, had prevented me from real love. My crush on Aaron was innocent, but I was too distracted by Israel to do anything about it anyway. I was busy learning my history.

Sometimes in class instead of drawing my name inside a heart, I'd draw it inside of a mini Israel. I had become skilled at sketching the country; I wrote the "L" in the west near Tel-Aviv, the "I" on top of Jerusalem, and the "Z" in the east near Jordan. We hadn't visited Jerusalem yet. I was getting antsy. It was our second week into the eight-week program. Jerusalem needed time; our teachers had much to tell us while the anticipation grew. One night on the campus after a long day of learning, Aaron attracted a crowd. He had discovered a eucalyptus tree whose leaves were, as Ornstein wrote, "lit by the moon beams" and was sitting under it with his guitar. He was singing the famous Naomi Shermer song, "Hurshat Ha'Eucalyptus" ("The Eucalyptus Grove"). After the song, he pulled some of the leaves off the tree and rolled them into a cigarette. I pushed my way past Maddie from Boca Raton—still wearing her Calvin Klein bright pink bikini from the afternoon's hike to the Galilee—to try to get closer to him. We passed the cigarette around like it was a joint. Aaron was serious about the land too, I could tell, as we both pulled the smoke—the land of Israel—from the cigarette inside of us.

The next week we were finally going to see Jerusalem. During class the morning before we boarded the bus, we read a section in Unit 2: Bayit Sheni (Second Temple) and Talmudic Periods. No author is cited for this passage from page 35, titled "16 Important Facts About Jerusalem":

> For three thousand years, the Jewish people have been inextricably bound to its capital, Jerusalem. This tie has been sustained through war, strife, persecution, exile, dispersion, and holocaust. In their darkest hours, Jews turned in prayer toward Jerusalem, for redemption. The twentieth century has witnessed both the rebirth of the Jewish state and the reunification of a sovereign Jewish capital in Jerusalem.

This claim to Jerusalem, I realize now, couldn't exist without victimhood. This tie between colonization and claiming victim space is even clearer in what follows:

> Yet the meaning of that rebirth and reunification has been little understood, and Jerusalem has become the centerpiece of political and military conflict involving states distant from Israel.

The marriage of power and victimhood that Israel has become was unbeknownst to me then. I believed tiny Israel to be a light unto the nations and thought everyone else in the world wanted to destroy her.

I was ready for the 45-minute ride up to Jerusalem. I entered the bus with my fanny pack strapped to my ripped and faded Levi shorts and my canteen across my shoulder. Some students, like Zach from New Jersey, filled their canteens with vodka. Aaron and I would roll our eyes at each other, annoyed. Aaron shook his head and we both scoffed at their immaturity. Aaron was so practical, I mused, as we both drank our water, hydrating ourselves for the sunny city. As we ascended towards the Jerusalem, I thought of Ornstein's description. Our skin, like the skin of the children of Israel she described, was also golden velvet from the sun's kisses.

When we entered Jerusalem from Highway 1 I was hooked. By the time we got to the Old City, I was in love. The smells of olives and za'atar and lemon and mint wafted through the corridors of the Old City like a fast rush-hour bustle, as the store owners—I knew they were Palestinians but they were like background to my idealist love affair with Israel—opened the doors of their shops and set their items out for the day. I relished stepping on stones we had studied about. We spent days walking the city. Each afternoon at the end of the day, the light would hit the stones of the Old City like the cheeks of a young girl blushing. The stone was a light rose—my name!—and I would squeeze my fists when no one was looking as I tried to make the dusk last. One shop owner gave me a dirty look when he saw me sitting, pausing, looking at the rose tinted stone. "Dumb American," he mumbled as he swept the garbage away in front of his shop. I thought the glow of the stone on my face made my skin look great.

That summer, when we were in Jerusalem, I would prefer to be alone than with others, even Aaron. I felt like Sarah Jessica Parker's character, Carrie, in "Sex in the City," walking proudly alone at the end of an episode late at night in the middle of a Manhattan street. She walks down the center of the road like she owns it. She doesn't need a man when she's got the city to spend time with.

A couple of weeks ago, when I told my student that I had gone on the same AMHSI program, his eyes widened and he looked at me differently. "I can't believe my teacher went on that program!" I heard him tell a friend as he left my classroom. "That's just so cool," he said in the hallway. He thinks we're bonded now, connected to the same lover. He'll do anything to protect his love, I can tell. I remember feeling this way too. During the teenage angst-filled years of high school, I enjoyed loving something so much larger than myself. I was living for something huge, and it felt selfless.

This is the brilliance of Israel, of course, that upper middle-class, spoiled, suburban, American teenagers can participate in the displacing of indigenous Palestinians, support an ongoing occupation, plant trees on Palestinian villages masked as parks, mystify the whole experience as love, and feel deeply in their souls that they're being selfless, working for a vision bigger than themselves. I had fallen in line as a good Zionist Jew and thought I had discovered it on my own. I'm behind now, learning what real love is, and understanding that the ideal as it was presented to me is really backdrop for walled-off cities that function as open-aired prisons, lack of water, movement, and dignity.

I did finally tell Aaron that I had a crush on him, but on the last day of our "eight week academic experience." I slipped him a note as we all said goodbye at the airport. He wrote me a letter a few weeks later once he was back in Boston. I was in Chicago, depressed, slogging through my senior year of high school. Loving Israel and plotting ways to go back helped me get through the year. I desperately wanted to return to Jerusalem for a gap year after I graduated. "Oh, no," my father balked. "You're going to college." I would get back to Jerusalem four years later, when Hebrew University would be the only graduate school I'd apply to. My father was excited about that. In Aaron's letter to me he said he had liked me, too, but that he was also shy. I seemed very focused, he said, and he wasn't sure if I'd be into him. "I should have told you," he wrote. "The summer could have been very different indeed." Aaron went on to become a cantor, and the last I heard, he was divorced and raising his daughter in New Jersey.

I remember when I scribbled a note to Amy from Miami during class. "I think I like someone in Galil," I wrote on the back of one of our units. It didn't matter though. Aaron wouldn't have had a chance with me. We were going to Jerusalem.

In the last several years, I've experienced a recurring dream about my paradigm shift from a Zionist to an anti-Zionist worldview. It feels like vertigo. I'm alone, maybe standing on a hill or mountain—a Judean mountain, perhaps?—and I can't look behind me. Everything I thought was real disappears. I'm nauseous. My knees buckle. I feel like I'm spinning as I finally understand Israel as Palestine. Not settlements, but all of it. Palestine. And then I know that young Jewish guys like Aaron, sitting under trees with long hair playing guitar didn't only happen the summer I was 16, but happen every summer Jews go to Israel and fall in love. They play the role perfectly in the farce without ever knowing they're performing. In the dream I realize that all of the experiences I thought had been real are all manufactured—a mask we all wear participating in the charade. We thought it was real, but it was all folly. Then, in the dream, I grasp Ilan Pappe's *The Ethnic Cleansing of Palestine* in one hand, Edward Said's *The Question of Palestine* in the other, and with a third hand—it's a dream, after all—Yitzhak Laor's *The Myths of Liberal Zionism*, and I jump.

    I found the booklets from attending AMHSI in 1986 a couple of years ago when I moved. They'd been sitting in the basement in a box labeled "Israel stuff." My student's excitement prompted me to look through them. Now, I'm so angry about the propaganda I mistook for truth, and I feel sad for the child I was who was fed this narrative as gospel. I was taught one-sided nonsense by those I loved and trusted the most.

    No one in our family was ever as passionate about Israel as me, and now I'm the most critical. My father can't deal with the swings. Sometimes I wonder if he hates who I've become, though he'd never admit it. I know it's been confusing for him, given how passionate he knew I was for Jerusalem when I was young. I begged him to support me. Now, as an adult watching him age, I want to beg him to understand me. I don't know if he'll be able to do it.

    Last week, when my student talked about Israel, he had the same glow I had when I was his age and had just returned from my first trip to Israel on the same program he'll be going on. Like me, he'll read Ornstein and Herzl and Ben-Gurion and Meir and Jabotinsky and all the others who will speak to what he knows is truth. As he talked about going next year, his face glowed like the stones of the Old City during dusk. I wonder about the relationships he'll have. It will be hard for anyone to measure up to that kind of love.

HOLY LAND HARPS

I waited until the tourists were about two feet away from our booth in the Jerusalem Convention Center to start playing the harp. Micah had told me to. My fingers were in position, poised, not yet touching the strings. The particular harp I played—Micah called it the Atara Nevel—was about two feet long; I sat on a wood stool, almost squatting, back straight, the harp resting between my knees, my legs pointed outwards to accommodate the instrument. It's important when playing the harp to have an open body posture. Micah said a relaxed body indicates a free mind, which one needs to let the music flow through you. The harp was made of ancient olive wood, hand carved by Micah himself. When I played the way Micah instructed, the tourists' heads turned towards me; I'd soon have them hooked.

This was the plan, of course, to play the harps and get Evangelical Christians to buy them. Thousands had descended on Jerusalem for the week from the U.S. for their 1994 annual pilgrimage. I can't remember the name of the conference, but I'm sure it included words like "Encounter" or "Summit" or "Forum."

The outside part of the harp bowed and curved up. When I played for the tourists, Micah instructed, my chin should be drawn upwards, too, so that it aligned with the top corner of the harp. "Your chin and the tip of the harp should be parallel," I'm sure he told me more than once, his long white hair falling behind his shoulders, the few times I was with him. I placed both wrists on either side of the harp, my right hand just an inch higher than the left. I had to make sure my fingertips brushed the strings gently, my hands relaxed and loose. As the tourists arrived, and they did, in droves, I caressed the strings like I was stroking a new lover's cheek for the first time, barely touching it. My face looked up towards the sky—or, in our case, the ceiling of the convention center—as I began strumming. Then I closed my eyes. The convergence of my fingers with the strings was divine. The sound reverberated and filled the space. The music became air itself—a soft and melodious cry, as though God himself was speaking through me.

We had arrived to Binyanei Ha'uma—its name in 1994, now it's called the Jerusalem Convention Center—hours before the Evangelicals came, to set up. Before heading to Jerusalem, the Evangelicals toured the small country, most for the first time. They visited the Church of the Nativity in Bethlehem—the current wall that surrounds the city wasn't built until 2000. They dunked themselves in the Sea of Galilee up north and afterwards ate lunch in nearby Tiberias. Once they arrived in Jerusalem, they visited the Church of the Holy Sepulchre and walked the 14 Stations of the Cross in the Christian Quarter of the Old City. They bought Christian trinkets in the shuk, the Arab market just inside Jaffa Gate, and it seemed, they would buy again, at the convention center booths. Until I worked the fair, I had little interaction with Evangelicals in Jerusalem. One of my friends, Sheryl, a grad student like me, had been working for Micah and asked if I wanted to help out with the "fair" to make some extra money. Micah had suggested we wear white robes, but I just couldn't do it. Instead, I wore a white skirt and a white tank top; I made 20 dollars for the day.

Micah and his wife Shoshanna Harrari are the owners of Harrari Harps, the only gallery-workshop in Israel that makes biblical harps. According to their website, the handcrafted harps are "Temple Quality Since 1984." The first harp Micah made was a birthday gift for Shoshanna—the name means rose in Hebrew and is my Hebrew name too. Shoshanna "was seeking an instrument to connect her soul to the true source of music," the shop site states, and also claims that Micah was the first person to make a harp in Israel in 2000 years. Each harp they construct is carefully crafted based on their research of ancient biblical harps, which also include "Talmudic writings and archeological findings." The harps have biblical names, too: Atara Nevel (the one I played at the Evangelical convention), Kinnor David, Kinnor Elijah, Davita, and King David. Wood choices include cherry, walnut, maple, cypress, rosewood, and olive. "Israeli olive," the site boasts, "is among the most ancient of our wood choices." Using native wood to build their harps is, in part, what makes them attractive to buyers. But olive wood has long been identified with Palestinian culture and livelihood, too, and over a million Palestinian olive trees have been destroyed by the Israeli government to make way for settlements and walls.

I'd seen Evangelicals before I worked the fair, moving in large groups around the ancient city wearing khaki pants, wide white hats, and newly-purchased gym shoes. They followed a leader who carried a bright pink umbrella. I was a 24-year-old Jewish American graduate student at Hebrew University and had been living in Jerusalem for two years. I was also dating Tavit. Together, we laughed at the tourists. Their presence helped me feel more grounded in the city I would make my home for five years before returning to Chicago. They stayed in hotels; I had an apartment. Tavit had a house in the Old City. Somewhere in between the tourists and Tavit, I stood, equidistant to these two extremes of temporary and permanent. Without the two poles I'd wobble. His friends owned shops where the Evangelicals bought their trinkets. Tavit's friends jacked up prices when the tourists arrived. I was a witness to their coming and going week by week as I stayed year after year. I was deeply in love with Jerusalem. I was in love with Tavit, too, and laughing with him at those who dabbled in the city for a week just deepened my connection to Jerusalem. I didn't have to work hard to love the city, though. Since I was a little girl, I had been told Israel was my birthright. No one had more claim than the Jews, preached family and friends. I had a sense of permanence for the city long before I ever visited.

Yet something inside me I could not name knew the land wasn't just for the Jews. Despite the messages I received growing up, I must have felt in my core something unsettling. Since those days, my Zionism has unraveled like an old sweater. One string was pulled when a seed was planted—perhaps on my first trip to the West Bank with Tavit when I began learning about the Palestinian narrative—and now, the whole sweater has since come apart.

One day, Tavit and I were in his friend Musaf's shop on the Via Dolorosa near the Church of the Holy Sepulchre. We sat on tiny wicker chairs and drank coffee from little glasses we rested on a round copper coffee table. We smoked a joint. I'm pretty sure it was late afternoon; I remember the western sun that day, like every day in Jerusalem towards the end of the afternoon, sharp and strong. All of a sudden we heard a noisy crowd. It wasn't uncommon to see tourists making their way down the Via Dolorosa but this was louder than usual. We looked out from inside the shop. Several people were walking behind and alongside a man with long hair who was hunched over wearing cream-colored shorts. The man walked in the middle of the narrow street. One of the people following him carried a camera; he was videotaping. On the man's back was a large wooden cross—I'll call him Jesus. Tavit, Musaf, and I stood in the doorway of the shop. Inside, copper swords and bronze necklaces hung on the walls. Out on the street a woman who walked next to the man with the camera said, "Do it again." I remember her face. She was irritated, like a frustrated director. "And try to look like you're suffering this time." Jesus walked back several feet, and, looking forlorn, carried the cross on his back once more. This time he bent his back forward more, wincing intensely, trying to look like he was in pain. Apparently this attempt still wasn't good enough, for the others appeared unhappy with Jesus's second performance. "We're done," the woman said. A few minutes later another Jesus tried out for the part. Tavit, Musaf, and I looked at one another, each with one foot inside the shop and the other foot outside on the street's stones, wobbling on the threshold of these two different worlds. Grabbing our bellies, we laughed so hard—I thought I must have just smoked really good weed—but Tavit said this happened sometimes, and it was just part of living in this crazy city.

I later learned that carrying a cross on the Via Dolorosa in Jerusalem is a common rite of passage for Christians—I didn't know. Like the actors, the Evangelical tourists I played the harp for at the fair were simply background scenery for those of us who were living and working in Jerusalem. We saw them as a pack, never as individuals. They existed in our minds only as "the Evangelicals," as though they were a single organism that breathed and moved as one.

Back when I worked at the fair at the Jerusalem Convention Center in 1994, Harrari Harps was located in downtown West Jerusalem, just off Yoel Solomon, a small pedestrian street with cafes, restaurants, and galleries. Their shop was tucked behind a hidden courtyard just behind Yoel Solomon, called Nachlat Shiva. Restaurants and shops dotted this tiny street, too, but they were less known, out of sight. When you'd amble down Nachlat Shiva, you'd feel as though you stumbled upon the small courtyard by accident, like you were the first to discover the artisan shops along the limestone alleyways that look as though they were built right into the ancient stone and curved arches.

Nachlat Shiva, which means "Inheritance of the Seven," was the third neighborhood built outside Jerusalem's Old City Walls. The phrase is a reference to the seven families who, as the story goes, in 1869 bought homes in the neighborhood in an effort to venture beyond the Old City. One of the neighborhood's first homes was bought by Yoel Solomon—for whom the pedestrian street adjacent to Nachlat Shiva is called. Solomon ran a printing press and his earliest publication was called HaShoshanna, a guidebook whose shape resembled a rose.

Once, while I was hanging out at Harrari Harps, Shoshanna tried to teach me how to play Bach's Minuet in G Major. A good friend, Miriam, was working at a bookstore-cafe in the same hidden courtyard a few doors down. The name of the cafe, Tmol Shilshom, Hebrew for "Only Yesterday," is the same name of a novel by S.Y. Agnon, the first Israeli writer to win the Nobel in Literature. When the bookstore opened in 1994, the year Miriam got a job there, Yehuda Amichai, Israel's greatest poet, read his poetry at the opening. Today, Tmol Shilshom is a literary hotspot in Jerusalem with regular readings and book events, tucked away into the small courtyard of Nachlat Shiva. Sometimes when I wasn't hanging out at the nearby Champs Bar around the corner on Yoel Solomon Street or at Harrari Harps in the courtyard, I did homework for my grad classes at Tmol Shilshom if Miriam was working that day. When her boss wasn't paying attention she'd bring me cheddar cheese sandwiches and fresh-squeezed orange juice. My favorite table was right next to a dark wood bookcase, its shelves built into an arched limestone wall.

The day Shoshanna Harrari showed me how to play Bach's Minuet in G Major, I clumsily plucked the strings with heavy fingers. I was trying to play the harp the same way I had played around with my brother's guitar years before—picking the strings hard out of insecurity. "Watch me," Shoshanna said. As though a spirit had just entered her body, she lifted her chin—I remember she had such lovely, tight skin—lowered her eyes, arched her back. Her toes, visible in her brown Naot sandals made in a factory up north in Israel, curled upwards as she ran her fingers across the harp. Though she barely touched the strings, the sound that emanated was full-bodied and penetrated the entire gallery. A couple weeks later, my friend Sheryl asked if I wanted to help out at the Evangelical fair.

The convention center is just across from the Central Bus Station on Jaffa Road. We set up the booth like the gallery itself. We put brightly-colored red and orange fabric on small tables to accentuate the different wood harps. Shoshannah brought a rug with blue and green stripes. Each harp was different and demanded a table appropriate to its height. Other booths sold Christian books, nativity scenes made from olive wood, anointing oil and oil lamps made up north near the Sea of Galilee. My task for the day was to put on a show for the Evangelicals, as I'd been coached, so they'd buy a harp.

It wasn't a sham, though, for Micah and Shoshannah. They sincerely believe the music from their homemade harps brings people closer to the holy land; they liken their harp-making to a calling. In a 2008 interview on Israel National Radio, Shoshannah explained that she and Micah had been wandering in the U.S. when they came across the Hebrew Bible. Quoting the Prophets, Shoshannah said God called his children from the four corners of the earth. "He will bring them back to their own land and He will replant them and never uproot them again," she recited. The Harraris felt they had a personal invitation from God to move to Israel. "And since we were Jewish, we're His children," she said.

According to the website, Micah isn't just a master craftsman. He's also a Levite, a descendent of one of the twelve tribes of Israel. The Levites assisted the priests in the ancient Jewish Temple. In addition to making harps for tourists, the Harraris also have a mission to prepare harps for when the Temple will be rebuilt in Jerusalem. Micah and Shoshannah's dedication to the rebuilding of the third Temple is so fierce that any cities mentioned on their site exist not in their current state, but as Biblical references. "The harp's gentle sound was even heard in far-away Jericho," for example. Today, Jericho is a Palestinian city in the West Bank. Aqbat Jabr and Ein el-Sultan, Palestinian refugee camps, border the Arab town. The location for the third Temple, should it ever be built, it's believed, is the Temple Mount in Jerusalem, the current location of the Dome of the Rock—one of Islam's holiest sites—built 691 A.D. Those who visit Micah and Shoshannah's website are invited to donate any amount for their "Temple Harp Project." The harps will reside at the Temple Institute of Jerusalem in the Old City for dedication, they say, where they will wait, with other harps, for the Temple to be rebuilt.

I suppose I should have felt bad masquerading at the fair, pretending to be a harp player for a few hours. I was complicit in perpetuating the Evangelicals' one-dimensional love for the city. I helped them view Jerusalem as the land of the Bible—a place of salvation where Christ will return. But I didn't feel bad. I enjoyed playing the harp that day, one eye on the instrument and the other watching their faces as they swooned at the sound. For, though I scoffed at the Evangelicals with a kind of moral superiority, I wasn't, ultimately, that much different from them when it came to my own love for Jerusalem. Judaism warns against proselytizing, but I had no problem telling the world why Israel was mine. Helping Christians feel a similar kind of love I felt only deepened my connection to Jerusalem. What did I care if some Christians came to the city for a week? They'd soon be back in their suburbs getting fat, driving their minivans and, maybe, learning to play a harp that would eventually collect dust on their living room mantel. Before I left Jerusalem in 1995, I bought my parents a harp from the Harrari's, too. It's a Davita, named for Chaim Potok's 1985 novel, *Davita's Harp*. It's made from Israeli rosewood. "From your Shoshannah," I wrote on the card when I gave it to them. It hangs on their living room wall, next to the mantel, collecting dust in their house in the suburbs.

It would be several more years until I would understand the historical relationship between Christian and Jewish Zionism, and the symbiotic effort to squeeze out any reference to the Palestinian lives and villages destroyed in 1948. Among Christian and Jewish Zionists, the Palestinians who continue, today, to live under Israel's military occupation—even those who are Christian—just don't come up. Most Christian Zionists believe that supporting a Jewish claim to the holy land is a prerequisite for the second-coming of Christ. Benjamin Netanyahu knows he needs Christian Zionist support because of their large numbers. According to the Pew Research Center, Evangelicals make up 26.3 percent of the population in the U.S., and most are Zionists. Jews make up just 1.8 percent. Addressing the Christians United for Israel's annual conference in 2017, Netanyahu told the Evangelical crowd that Israel has "no greater friends than Christian supporters of Israel." Netanyahu's pandering makes sense given the large numbers—and to ensure the support he needs, he is willing to sell his Jewish soul.

I read on the website that the Harrari's gallery-workshop is now located in the moshav Ramat Raziel, a small Israeli cooperative about 17 kilometers west of Jerusalem. I wondered if they still had their shop in Nachlat Shiva too. Their email address is listed on the site, so I decided to write them and ask. Shoshannah replied to my inquiry a few days later. She didn't remember me, but she did recall my friend Sheryl who had worked for her, the one who had gotten me the day-long gig at the Evangelical fair. They moved their shop to the moshav, she wrote, so they can work where they live. She was tired of commuting to Jerusalem; she thinks the former gallery in Nachlat Shiva is now a restaurant.

Moshav Ramat Raziel was established in 1948, the same year Israel became a state. It's just off Highway 395—a road known for its 20 kilometers of limestone ruins and pine tree forests that winds through the Jerusalem hills, the same hills where Palestinian villages were destroyed in 1948. For over a century, the Jewish National Fund has been planting trees in Israel to cover up remains of these villages—except, perhaps, a few remnants like a cistern or a terrace, so that visitors to the area can marvel at the "biblical ancient ruins." When I was a girl, I saved my allowance money to plant a tree in Israel. It was a selfless act, I was taught.

Decades later—once I knew—I drove through the forests on the way to Jerusalem from the airport and became sick. I had read about Israel's efforts to cover up the destruction of Palestinian life and culture and history, and how they got young Zionists like me to pay for it. As a little girl, I was proud to have planted a tree; I still have the certificate that was sent to me. A small child with brown pigtails digs into the earth with a shovel, the tree a primary green, bright, like green M&Ms.

Moshav Ramat Raziel is on the ruins of the Palestinian village, Kasla. The village was destroyed on July 17, 1948, in an operation called Operation Dani by the Harel Brigade. Ramat Raziel is named for David Raziel, a commander of the Irgun, a Zionist underground paramilitary organization whose mission was to "depopulate" Palestinian villages in 1948. Before it was destroyed, Kasla had 78 homes. Three-hundred-thirty people lived in the village. Palestine Remembered and Zochrot, two organizations that research and document Palestinian life before 1948, report that Kasla's location is identified with Chesalon, a first-century Canaanite city. The village thrived. Palestinian life existed. Sixty-one people lived in Kasla in 1596. In the nineteenth century, two springs provided fresh water for the village. Kasla's villagers planted olives, fruit, and grain in the lowlands. Crops drank the rain, irrigated from the springs. The villagers were Muslim. I read that almond trees grow on top of the mountain, cactuses along the southern slopes. Shoshannah's email finished as warmly as it began. "Here we are out in the forest," she wrote, "a different kind of beauty." She ended her email with "Blessings," and I was sure that she meant it.

"Rose-Red City Half as Old as Time"

The desert mountains were beige and gray and huge and looked like the moon. It appeared as though they were moving alongside our bus, just more slowly—guarding us, perhaps, from something larger and unbeknownst to us at the time—but of course it was us, not the mountains, that were in motion. We were zigzagging our way at 40 miles an hour through the windy roads of the Negev desert from the inside of an air-conditioned bus. Scott, my ex-boyfriend, had been dozing pretty much the whole ride from Jerusalem down to Eilat, the southern tip of Israel that sits on the Red Sea. I took breaks from reading my *Lonely Planet* guidebook to stare out the window. At one point I tilted my head to try to see the tops of the mountains, almost bumping into Scott's shoulder—a pool of drool had accumulated at the side of his open mouth as he slept—but I couldn't see their peaks. Others were sleeping on the bus, too. Except for a baby who cried on and off it was mostly quiet. I was pretty sure a young couple was fooling around in the back of the bus, alternating between giggling and moaning. I looked at Scott. I was angry he was missing the desert view. "I'm just along for the ride," he'd said an hour earlier. For a few seconds I watched him sleep and knew I couldn't love him the way he wanted me to.

We were on our way to Amman, Jordan, then Petra, then back down to Egypt before returning to Jerusalem. Once we arrived to Eilat, we crossed over to Aqaba, then took another bus back up north to Amman. I had been living in Jerusalem for a few years as a graduate student at Hebrew University when I received Scott's letter saying he was coming to Israel. I wasn't excited about the trip; which is to say, I was looking forward to traveling to two countries I'd never visited before, but not necessarily with Scott. We had dated for a year several years back when I was a junior in college in Madison, Wisconsin. It was an anti-climactic breakup. I just didn't really like him. He annoyed and bored me.

Three years later, after no contact, I received the letter from Scott saying he was coming to Israel to visit family. "If you're free when I'm there," he wrote, "maybe we can go somewhere together." He happened to be arriving during my semester break from the university—later, I'd wonder if this had been on purpose since he knew I'd be on break. I had been wanting to visit Jordan and Egypt so I suggested we go together. It was 1994, just six months after Israel and Jordan signed the peace treaty—people could finally enter from Israel. I watched the signing on Israeli TV. I was doing some editing and translating work for an elderly man in Jerusalem's Katamon neighborhood the day of the treaty and we watched it together in his living room and drank mint tea. My boss lived on Palmach Street, a short walk from my apartment which was across the street from the Jerusalem Theatre on Chopin Street.

We had not been able to take a linear route from Jerusalem to Amman because the Allenby Bridge, which we would have taken from Israel into Jordan, hadn't yet reopened. It was December, and Jordan and Israel had only signed the peace treaty in October. We called the bridge Gesher Allenby because that's what Israelis call it. In Arabic it's called Al-Karameh, the bridge Palestinians use to leave the West Bank. Jordanians call it the King Hussein Bridge. Shortly after the peace treaty, a new modern crossing was built next to the older one with help from the Japanese Government. The distance between Amman and Jerusalem is only 157 miles, but because we couldn't use the bridge, we had to take a bus from Jerusalem 192 miles down south to Eilat, cross over into Aqaba, and then take another bus back up north 202 miles back to Amman.

I didn't plan the trip well. It made sense for me to go during my semester break, of course, but I didn't realize until we were already on the bus that it was Ramadan, the Muslim holiday where strict fasting is observed from sunrise to sunset for about a month. In certain cities, eating and drinking in public is forbidden. Jordan is roughly 94 percent Muslim and about 70 percent Palestinian. Most of the two million Palestinians who live in Jordan came as refugees, or from families of refugees, from Israel between 1947 and 1967. About 370,000 live in refugee camps inside Jordan.

We left Jerusalem at 7:00 am and had been traveling the whole day, so by the time we had crossed over into Aqaba and headed back up north towards Amman, it was just after sundown. We were the only Americans on the bus. All of a sudden, everyone around us started drinking water out of gallon-sized milk cartons and lighting cigarettes. They'd take a long swig with their eyes closed, the cold water rushing down their throat, deep into their organs as though it contained a special life-force, then would pass the cartons to the next person. When one came to me, I smiled graciously, stupidly, trying to pretend I was familiar with this ritual. They deeply inhaled their cigarettes too. As a young twenty-something living abroad, I had no problem joining them in this ritual, though when I smoked, it was with bravado. Then I wondered how we were going to find food during the day on this trip.

We arrived at the youth hostel in Amman in the early evening, and we crashed from the long day of travel. In the morning, I woke up before Scott did and read about the ancient Roman amphitheatre, our first stop in the city, in my *Lonely Planet* book. We drank some instant coffee in the hostel lobby, which wasn't really a lobby, more like a couple of beaten-down brown chairs in a small room with peeling teal and orange paint, a black kettle on a counter for hot water. The instant coffee seemed an attempt by the hotel owners to keep the tourists happy but not coddled. They'd hydrate us, they figured, even during Ramadan, but our search for food wasn't their problem. Luckily I hadn't thrown away the bruised tangerine and crusty bread I had brought with me from Jerusalem the day before. I shared some with Scott and we got a taxi.

I read that Amman's old Roman amphitheatre is cut into the northern part of a hill so that the sun doesn't disturb the spectators. It sits low and rises up as you near it, which I could see from the cab as we got closer. I tried not to look at Scott when we were in the taxi because he looked bored again—he had just yawned loudly enough for the cab driver to hear—and it made me angry.

    Beyond these things that annoyed me, Scott was a normal guy, and for some reason I wasn't aware of at the time, this irritated me too. He deserved to be with someone who was in love with him. He wanted—someday, "down the road," he'd say—to get married and buy a house and have kids. I was sure that on the weekends he'd want to invite other couples over with their kids for dinner—a BBQ in the backyard, of course, with red-checkered plastic tablecloths—that you make with all the cutlery you got as gifts from your wedding registry, and take family road trips and have spontaneous teachable moments where your kids learn some lesson, like that bad people exist in the world but you always want to still try to be good nonetheless, or some such nonsense like that, where you feel really self-satisfied about your parenting when you put your kids to sleep that night, though you'd never say so. You just do all the things that normal people do. I was raised in a family that taught me I should strive for such normalcy, too, but something about it made me feel claustrophobic and restless. I might have been projecting onto him because I didn't really know what exactly he wanted. Or perhaps I was simply aggravated by Scott and might have wanted those things with someone else—I can't remember now. What I had called normal was simply another way of saying it was just what the majority of people did, what the girls I knew dreamt about from an early age. For whatever reason, I just didn't want it. So on a Thursday afternoon in Madison after watching *All My Children*, I told Scott we should break up. He got upset and moved, rather quickly it seemed at the time, from anger to detached indifference. We left my apartment together and then walked down State Street in opposite directions. I went to Pizza Hut and ate greasy breadsticks with an extra side of tomato sauce. That evening, I called my mother crying, worried that I'd always be alone. She didn't know what to say, so instead she asked me if I had caught the split-infinitive on that day's episode of *All My Children*—resorting, as she often did as an English teacher, to her joy of finding grammar mistakes on television shows. "It was a good one," she chuckled.

Boxy, white, Arab-style houses dotted the hills around the amphitheatre. Built in the 2nd century when the area was called Philadelphia, the amphitheatre seats 6000 and is built on three tiers. The acoustics are supposed to be so good that if you stand towards the top rows, it's believed you can hear the people on stage even if they whisper. As soon as we got there, I made my way down the steep stairs towards the stage. Scott sat on one of the rows towards the top. As I walked down the sharp steps of the amphitheatre, my mind flashed back to a memory of the stairs in Anne Frank's house in Amsterdam when my father brought me in 1985. My parents couldn't afford for our family of five to travel abroad together, so he took turns bringing one of us three kids at a time when he went for work. He had a conference in Brussels and we took the train to Amsterdam for the day. I got the chills as we walked up the stairs just behind the bookcase that hid the stairway. A few minutes before we had stood on the corner of Rozengracht and Keizersgracht Streets, not far from Anne Frank's house on Prinsengracht. He gave me the map and said, "Figure out how we get there." He was patient as I found our way. We walked up Rozengracht, a left on Prinsengracht, and down a few blocks. It was a small walk for sure, but that afternoon I learned to use a map.

The highest rows in the amphitheatre, though farthest from the stage, not only have great acoustics but also have excellent sightlines of both the stage and the city of Amman. It seems to be a place where people come to hang out, like a park—a quiet respite in a big city. A man read a book lying down on one of the rows, his backpack under his head like a pillow. Two women sat together looking down at the stage, not talking. A boy walked up and down the stairs several times methodically and determined while his father talked to a friend. A group of tourists followed a man who held a pink umbrella. Sitting on the top rows, I felt lifted out of the busy bustle of the everyday. The morning light was a soft blush and the sun spread itself over the ancient rock as it made its way around the amphitheatre. I was overwhelmed with how the light hit the stone in Jerusalem and I walked up and down the steps a couple times like the little boy I had watched earlier. Then I stood on the stage trying to absorb the theatre's massiveness.

"By chance, are you headed to Petra?" someone asked me on the stage. His name was Diego, and as he spoke he adjusted his silver wiry glasses behind his thick black hair to make sure he could see. He had a round beer belly, his gray The Who t-shirt tight around his midsection.

"By chance, I am!" I answered sprightly, awkwardly, more eager than I would have liked to have sounded. Diego was from Peru—he was studying in Boston and visiting the Middle East and Africa during his break. He seemed to possess an appropriate amount of nerdiness, which I was immediately drawn to.

"We should go together," he suggested. He had a confidence that indicated he knew the rules of travel. It was okay to ask a stranger, even a male, to travel together because it was under the guise of simply getting where you needed to go. "It'll be cheaper," he said, tucking his hair behind his ears, scanning the magnificence of the ampitheatre.

This is what is supposed to happen when you travel, I'm sure I thought at the time. You meet cool people and the next thing you know, you're traveling with them across a foreign country. Travel allowed me to pretend I was someone else. I could imagine I was easy-going, carefree, one of those hippie girls I envied at the Jewish summer camp I attended and who were on my first trip to Israel, who wore long prairie skirts they found at second-hand stores. Just like the Dylan song, they wore silver bracelets on their wrists and flowers in their hair. They had an intentionally messy side braid and somehow the flowers didn't fall out. They were light and airy, flitting down the hallway with their Birkenstock sandals and thick mix-matched socks. You know girls like these, don't you? They have that perfect skin and wet, full lips that never require lipgloss and they don't need glasses. They might have a sexy brown mole on their cheek. They make large dinners for their friends. Their glassware is random, also from second-hand stores, but all of it together preciously just seems to match. They spend hours at the farmer's market buying just the right kind of baby bok choy—full, not too skinny—for their dinner. They walk up to you so gracefully and take your crown of thorns. *Come in*, they say, and give you shelter from the storm. At the time, I couldn't really explain the heaviness I felt I carried around with me and when I was around those girls I just felt myself fall short.

"Why not?" I answered Diego. And just like that, I had another travel partner and could pretend, briefly, I was one of those girls.

When you travel, you connect with people more quickly than in your everyday life. I met someone while eating alone in a restaurant in Ljubljana, watching the sunset on the beach in Tel-Aviv, in line for a ticket at the train station in Paris, standing on a bridge in Venice. That just didn't happen to me in Chicago. So meeting someone standing on a stage in a Roman amphitheatre in Jordan became no big deal; by which I mean, I could act like it wasn't a big deal. And when it does occur, you step outside yourself for a moment, and you think what a great, enviable story it will be when you tell your friends that you met someone standing on a stage in a Roman amphitheatre in Jordan—but you don't show it. And for just that moment, when I met Diego, I believed that I was living an envious life, that for a few days I was the kind of person who easily just met people. Light and breezy.

Living abroad in Jerusalem allowed me to live in two worlds—I could be a tourist, but I also was working and studying in another country I could call home. I scoffed with superiority at the travelers who came for just a week. The little green piece of paper stuck inside my passport was all the proof I needed: I was more than a tourist but not a citizen—a faux expat on a student visa. Though I was living in Israel, I didn't know what it was like to work full time, serve in the army, pay taxes. I was just another well-educated, upper middle-class Jew, a good liberal Zionist who had dreamed of living in Israel. Most of my friends at the time, other Zionists studying in Israel, returned to the U.S. a few years later, got full time jobs, bought cars and property, moved to the suburbs—surely held their BBQ dinners in their backyard with the red-checkered tablecloths—had kids and got fat. They were good at small talk at parties. They represented some kind of upper middle-class post-college success in the U.S. that I just didn't want, or wasn't good at. But Scott wanted this kind of life, and for some reason, he wanted it with me.

As Diego and I made our way up to where Scott was sitting—he hadn't moved from the upper row—I introduced them and told Scott Diego's idea for the three of us to go to Petra together. Scott said, "Sure," and shook Diego's hand. I couldn't tell if he was annoyed or just didn't care. Diego reached into his bag and offered us some bread. Of course, I thought to myself, unlike Scott and me, he had prepared for Ramadan. It was late morning. We agreed to get our stuff from the hostel and meet in the center of town in a couple hours to catch a taxi to Petra.

The taxi driver, Ahmed, chain-smoked as he drove, even though it was in the middle of the afternoon. He spoke a little English, and told us you're not supposed to smoke during the day when it's Ramadan, which we knew. But we soon understood he was telling us because he would need our help if the police happened to drive by. If he was caught smoking during the day, he said he could be fined, or worse, thrown in jail for the remainder of Ramadan. In a short while a police car did pass by, and Ahmed tossed his cigarette over his shoulder to where we sat in the back seat. I was in the middle between Diego and Scott. I caught the cigarette and held it down between my knees until the police passed.

Ahmed had taken Desert Highway Route 15 from Amman to Petra, a road that like its name, cuts right through the hilly desert. The windows were open during the three-hour drive and the sound of the wind cutting through the glass at times made it too loud to talk, but I didn't mind. The sand-colored hills in the distance starkly juxtaposed with the power lines that lined the road. We were hungry, but we didn't want to tell Ahmed. Although he was smoking, we didn't want to assume he was also eating. But after about an hour and a half—midway to Petra—Ahmed pulled off the road onto a gravel driveway near a gas station. I assumed he needed to fill the car with gas. He parked and motioned for us to get out. Diego and I looked at each other. Scott shrugged. We entered a small room with low ceilings just behind the gas station. About 10 people sat on the floor around a low table. Ahmed seemed to know them all and hugged a few of the men. Everyone was smoking cigarettes. Along with the nicotine, smells of lemon and garlic and mint filled the room. An orange and yellow tablecloth covered the wood table. At least twenty different small plates were on the table: fresh hummus, smoked baba ganoush, tahini with parsley, tahini with tomatoes and cucumbers, falafel, yogurt and garlic, tomatoes and garlic, olive oil and za'atar, olives, radishes, grape leaves, tabbouleh, all on tiny plates covering the table. Our host tossed warm pita to each person like a frisbee, throwing them as soon as they were warm and crispy on the heater. Someone offered us cigarettes. "What a way to subvert Ramadan," Diego whispered closely in my ear as we ate and smoked with the others. When we left, our hosts packed us some pita bread and hummus. Back in the taxi, Ahmed, satisfied, tossed the toothpick he had been using to clean his teeth out the window.

By the time we arrived to Petra, it was too late to walk around. We found a youth hostel nearby but it was expensive. Jordan was seeing a large increase in Israeli tourism since the peace treaty. Diego asked if we three could share the room to save money. Scott was annoyed but agreed. Our room had three single beds. Diego asked to read my *Lonely Planet* book—"to make sure I am prepared for Petra tomorrow"—and soon was engrossed in his reading. Scott joined me in my bed and we fooled around. When Scott kissed my neck, I looked over at Diego, who by then had fallen asleep, the book on his round belly, his glasses resting low on his nose. Scott was the most excited I'd seen him all day. I feigned interest—a pathetic attempt at solicitude. I felt bad he'd come all this way. He should get something out of being here, I thought at the time. It wasn't his fault I wasn't in love with him. We were quiet so Diego wouldn't hear us.

The next morning we finished the pita and hummus our hosts had given us the day before at the secret lunch and walked to Petra. "Part of the continuing allure of the 'rose-red city,'" Diego read aloud from the book as we entered the town, adjusting his glasses as he read, "is that Petra still has many secrets yet to be discovered." Petra is also called the "Pink City," he told us enthusiastically, because of the rose-colored rock. Later, he asked me if he could borrow the book after we left Petra. He was going to continue traveling around Jordan before heading to Africa, he said. He promised to send it back to me when he returned to Boston. In Petra, we were early enough to see the morning light reflect the sandstone buildings as we entered.

The limestone buildings in Jerusalem turn a rosy color when the afternoon sun hits the rock but the sandstone in Petra is a deep mauve streaked with orange and brown. It reminded me of when I was young and my mother had just had back surgery for her spinal stenosis. Once she was in recovery, the surgeon described the image of the blood rushing into places where it had been restricted for years. "When the blood started flowing into these gray areas," he said, "it looked like a vibrant sunset swirling in her spine." In Petra, speechless, we stood in silent awe at the streaked rosy rock. There are about 800 sights to see and we only got to a few: The Siq, the 1.2 kilometer entrance to Petra which is like a long narrow gorge; Al Khazneh, the Treasury, the best preserved building in Petra; the Ad-Deir monastery. Depending on the time of the day, the stone looks peach, rose-petal pink, blood-orange red. Later, the yellow sun became more diluted with each minute as it fell quickly behind the mountains, west towards Israel. In a few minutes, I remember thinking, the sun would glisten on the Mediterranean as it dipped into the sea—a view forbidden to so many Palestinians.

As it turned dark, we headed back to the hostel to collect our things. We said goodbye to Diego. He headed North as we headed South, back towards Egypt. Six months later, as promised, I received a small package in the mail. It was from Diego who was back in Boston. I would never hear from him again. On the inside flap of the *Lonely Planet* book, he had written a note of thanks. On another page, he had copied a sonnet by hand, written by John Burgon in 1845, titled "Petra":

> It seems no work of Man's creative hand,
>
> by labour wrought as wavering fancy planned;
>
> But from the rock as if by magic grown,
>
> eternal, silent, beautiful, alone!
>
> Not virgin-white like that old Doric shrine,
>
> where erst Athena held her rites divine;
>
> Not saintly-grey, like many a minster fane,

that crowns the hill and consecrates the plain;

But rose-red as if the blush of dawn,

that first beheld them were not yet withdrawn;

The hues of youth upon a brow of woe,

which Man deemed old two thousand years ago,

match me such marvel save in Eastern clime,

a rose-red city half as old as time.

By the time I received the book, I had moved apartments and was living on Palmach Street, just around the corner from my former apartment on Chopin. I had met Tavit and would soon fall deeply in love with him. Later, I'd reject my Zionism, and would remain in love during the next two years while finishing my studies in Jerusalem.

After another frustrating day of travel we arrived in Cairo. When we got to the hotel, I told Scott I wanted to walk around by myself. I was annoyed that it was just the two of us again—Diego had been a nice distraction. I told Scott I needed some time to myself, and I went for a walk along the Nile River. Later, once I returned to the hotel, I suggested we walk through the Khan El-Khalili market—believed to be the oldest open-air market in the Middle East. Small boys carried large trays of fresh pita bread that smelled like za'atar on their heads. Shop owners stood outside their stores trying to sell sweet perfume. By the time we got back to the hotel, I had decided to cut the trip short. I had no reason to give Scott. It was just time to go. We agreed to see the Sphinx and pyramids before heading to the bus station to go back to Jerusalem. We checked out of the hotel and took a taxi the 13 kilometers to Giza.

As I looked in front of us in the cab, all of a sudden I saw three tiny triangles in the distance that grew as we got closer. Soon I saw the Sphinx too. The scene looked more like a photo than the real thing. When we exited the taxi boys on donkeys swarmed us, trying to sell us pictures and bracelets. I was unaware of the extent of these kids' poverty and of our privilege. I blamed Scott they'd bothered us since he looked like an American tourist more than I did, but that wasn't fair to him. It was windy as we walked around. The three pyramids, Khufu, Khafre, and Menkaure, each have square bases representing the four directions. The temples inside the pyramids face east. The Sphinx faces east, too, and is oriented, accordingly, with the sunrise. You can pay for a ticket to enter the pyramids, but we didn't. I'm not sure now why, but I'm assuming we both were just ready to leave. You can touch the Pyramids but not the Sphinx. We got as close as we could. My neck cracked as I bent my head to look up.

Before we left Giza to head back to Israel, Scott touched my shoulders and turned me to him, away from the Sphinx. I was surprised by his intensity.

"Come home from Israel as soon as you finish your degree," he said, pulling me closer. "Move in with me. Let's get married." He'd been building to this. The sand shifted between my toes in my brown sandals. The wind was hot, dry. The few tourists I saw seemed to keep to themselves. The light had begun to fade and all I saw was beige—the sand, the stone of the ancient bedrock buildings, Scott's khaki pants. I took it personally when the sand whipped at my cheeks and stung my eyes. My insignificance among these buildings, most of them nearly five thousand years old, was palpable. The scene was far too spectacular—it made what was happening between Scott and me all the more trivial.

It took me less than a minute to know how I would respond to Scott, but the moment lingered and hovered above us. I felt heavy, the opposite of an easy-going hippie girl. I knew it was going to be a terribly long trip back to Jerusalem, that I'd never hear from Scott again once he returned to the U.S. My mind began to drift. My desire to escape what was expected of me back home had created a restlessness in me. I wondered if one day in the future this moment would become meaningful to me, if I'd look back on it with nostalgia, if I was capable, ultimately, of experiencing real love; for how many chances, I wondered, does a person get in a lifetime? Scott looked at me waiting for my answer. I tried to think about the meaning of this trip, indeed the meaning of my life, of the potential future trips I might make with other men, perhaps in other places and in other times, but I came up short. I didn't know.

"I don't think so," I winced. Scott's lips pinched. He couldn't have been surprised, I thought. I hadn't treated him well. My eyes started to burn from the sand and then began to water. I looked towards the pyramids and the Sphinx. Scott was blocking my view. I wanted to see them in their entirety again before we left. But the scene of everything around me was warped, skewed. I rubbed my eyes and blinked, and took another look before we left.

It's Their Birthright

It would be a lie to say I wasn't deeply moved when the 947 bus pulled into Jerusalem as dusk descended on the golden city on Christmas Day. Who wouldn't be stirred by the dramatic ascent into a town bathed in limestone. It's always been this way for me. And though I'm no longer a Zionist, I remember most strongly what it feels like to be one at that moment I cross the threshold into the city.

Earlier that day, I spent Christmas morning with participants from Taglit Birthright, the free trip to Israel for Jews under age 32 who were attending one of the new study abroad Birthright trips, Israeli Multiculturalism, from December 24 - January 6. I met them at Kibbutz Afik, a collective community in the southern Golan Heights. Afik was established in 1972 by Israelis who did their military service in the Golan Heights and helped Israel occupy the land from Syria in 1967. Today, about 250 people live in the kibbutz.

In 2018, Birthright began offering these academic study abroad programs to U.S. college students. Now, in addition to getting a free trip, students can earn three college credits. Taglit Birthright partners with several different organizations like Sachlav, Hillel International, Mayanot, Rothberg International School of the Hebrew University of Jerusalem, and Hinam, the

Center for Social Tolerance—an encounter program that "promotes acquaintance" between Arab and Jewish citizens of Israel through principles like "colorblindness" and a "positive attitude," according to their About Us page.

The academic-themed courses Birthright offers are—Eco-Israel: Sustainability and Conservation, Food and Wine of Israel, Archeology: Uncovering the Hidden Past, Conflict Management & Counter-Terrorism, Innovation and Entrepreneurship, Diplomacy in the New Middle East, and Israeli Multiculturalism. At the end of the program, students have two weeks to write a 7-9 page paper that is graded by a professor contracted with Birthright. For just 250 U.S. dollars, the three credits can be transferred to the student's college. Given that three-credit courses at colleges can cost students thousands of dollars, the Birthright Israel Study Abroad program is a heck of a deal.

I was able to get hold of the Birthright course outline from one of the chaperones. According to the syllabus, the course focuses on five groups that contribute to Israel's multicultural society: the LGBTQ community, the Ethiopian community, members of the settlement movement, the Ultra-Orthodox community, and the Arab community.

Part One of the Course Unit on "Arab Society" refers to the "Israeli-Arab Citizens" who live within Israel and is notably ambiguous:

> Approximately one fifth of the residents of the State of Israel are Arab. In a State that is defined as 'Jewish Democratic' they are left with questions of meaning that affect their position and integration into 'The Jewish State'. We will learn about the characteristics of Arab society from different viewpoints and religious traditions, such as the Arab community, family and culture.

Some of these "different viewpoints" and "religious traditions" are broken down into smaller unit topics within Arab society such as Culture and

Folklore, Women in the Arab-Israeli society, The Culture of Food, Village Life, and the Muslim religion.

To an outside observer, the syllabus does indeed look like Birthright is tackling these complex multicultural issues within Israeli society. Under "Culture and Folklore", for example, it states that students will "learn the Arabic dance 'Davka' and its place in culture and community events." (The dance was spelled "Davka" and not the Arabic "Dabka".) Students learn the dance without actually learning its history from the Palestinian perspective. They don't, for instance, learn about the power imbalance between the Palestinian citizens of Israel and Jewish Israelis, or about the Palestinians living in the West Bank and Gaza. They don't learn about the Palestinian villages that were destroyed in 1948. The "Israeli-Arabs" are never called Palestinians, and the word Palestine is never used. Birthright's idea of multiculturalism then becomes a form of entertainment rather than a discussion of institutional power and Palestinian history.

Part Two of the Course Unit on "Arab Society" is titled the "The Arab-Israeli Conflict." Unit topics include: The Gaza Strip and its surrounding settlements, The ethics of Masada and its place in Zionism, David Ben Gurion as a visionary, and History of the establishment of the State of Israel and its wars.

Again, it appears that Birthright is tackling these complex issues, but ultimately the syllabus is apolitical in how the "Conflict" is described:

> The Arab society in Israel finds itself in constant tension. On the one hand Arab individuals owe loyalty to the State of Israel as citizens but on the other hand, they have family ties and a common culture and nationality with the Arab World, which has been embroiled in a long and historical conflict with the State of Israel. In order to understand their unique situation, we will survey the Jewish-Arab conflict from its roots, up until recent times.

The only "constant tension" here is the one Arabs have between their "loyalty" to the Jewish state and their connection to the larger "Arab world." Students are told they will study the conflict "from its roots," that any "tension" the Arabs experience is because of this torn loyalty. Arabs are portrayed here as passive subjects of another people's history, absorbed into Israel. Students don't learn about the 1948 Nakba from the Palestinian perspective, that the land was Palestinian, that it was taken and colonized by Israel. Birthright's version of multiculturalism both ignores Palestinian history and exploits its "Arab culture," so that it appears exotic. Palestinian history is pointedly left out.

One could argue that students do learn about the Palestinians in Gaza in "The Gaza Strip and its surrounding settlements" section, but only insofar as it serves to perpetuate Israel's role as victim:

> A case study of the Gaza Strip and its Israeli perimeter in the Arab-Israeli conflict. We will get acquainted with the history of the conflict, the Jewish residents of the villages bordering the Gaza perimeter and the missile attacks against them, and Hamas dominance in the area.

Israel is represented as minding its own business, just trying to survive. Students are told they will talk with the Jewish residents near Gaza, but they won't speak with Gazans or hear their perspective. They won't learn about the peaceful Friday protests, for example, or the humanitarian crisis of Gaza that Israel has created.

These evasions and distortions in the Birthright syllabus are dangerous because the "Arab history" students are getting could sound legitimate to some who don't know much about the conflict.

But a closer look reveals a sophisticated insidiousness that not only exploits the very Palestinians who are ignored, but also exploits the students who have come on the trip to learn something. The Israeli Multiculturalism syllabus is manipulative; students are presented with a course that claims to represent Israel's diversity but ultimately does nothing more than subtly perpetuate the erasure of Palestinian life while lauding Israel. That students visit David Ben Gurion's home and read his "vision of Israeli society," for instance, as described in the unit topic, "David Ben Gurion as a visionary,"—listed under the Arab-Israeli Conflict heading!—shows that the Birthright curriculum was written with the intention of making sure only Israeli history is presented and celebrated.

I'm not trying to suggest that the Birthright students are passive. Certainly they can choose to learn more about Palestine, as indeed some have. But as a teacher, I also know what it's like to wield power over a room of eager students. How I present information matters.

At my previous school, when I was a new teacher we held an annual "International Night," where students brought foods and wore clothes representative of their culture and tradition. It was a lovely evening celebrating the school's multicultural student body, and the food, as you can imagine, was amazing. But a couple years later it occurred to me, as I began reading about power and seeing the power imbalances among the student population within my own classroom, that it is important to talk about power—who has it and how it's used to coerce and oppress. I teach high school and it's incumbent on me to teach my students to think critically. Certainly the older college students who attend Birthright study abroad trips—who are studying at top U.S. universities—deserve to receive an education that encourages them to think critically, too, and does not only present a version of history that ignores and exoticizes others while making sure Israel looks good.

Even the kibbutz the Birthright participants visited both ignores and exoticizes the Syrian history it erased so that the kibbutz can be marketed as simultaneously ancient and modern. According to its website, Kibbutz Afik has a spa with 50 rooms of "country lodging," and "a spectacular, panoramic view of the Sea of Galilee." Treat yourself to a massage or swim in the pool, the site boasts, and "enjoy historical sites such as the aqueduct by the spring, which the Syrians used to water the nearby orchard." Here, Israel erases Syrian history in the Golan, but also fetishizes it as background scenery for current Israeli life on the kibbutz. The Roman historical sites are commodified and appropriated so that Kibbutz Afik can brand itself as both timeless and timely while the Syrian people who did live there remain passive and ignored—they were there but not there.

If the Birthright college students received a true history of the kibbutz they visited, they would also learn that Kibbutz Afik is on stolen Syrian land. The Syrian town was called Fiq. In 1967 it had a population of 2,800. After the 1967 war, it was evacuated.

Of course, the ways Israel ignores and fetishizes Palestinian culture isn't confined only to Birthright classes. As I walked around Jerusalem's Rehavia neighborhood the day after I took the bus into the city, I saw an advertisement for a "Stunning Authentic Arab house" for sale in the German Colony neighborhood—an example of Israel sentimentalizing the past while it both fetishizes and ignores Palestinian history. The Israeli real-estate company advertises the house as "Arab," which for potential homeowners means that it is ancient. Here "Arab" is only a style, a type of house with gorgeous arches and ancient tiles. The commodification becomes one more marketing opportunity for high-end Israeli real-estate to cover up Palestinian history at the same time being dependent on it to further its own agenda. The Palestinians remain anonymous—from there but not from there.

The same afternoon, I walked around the construction site for the new Museum of Tolerance near the City Center, a development sponsored by the Simon Wiesenthal Center. The site sits on the historic 600-year-old Muslim Mamilla cemetery. Many of the tombs have been destroyed and construction has been halted several times due to the controversy of building the museum on the cemetery. In 2010, architect Frank Gehry withdrew from the project because the project included destroying Muslim graves, yet the Wiesenthal Center maintains the importance of "building in Jerusalem because the Museum's principal themes of universal respect, Jewish unity, and coexistence are absolutely vital to Israel's future." I walked through the cemetery, noting the Arabic writing on some of the graves that have not been touched.

Later, I asked Tavit to translate the headstone of one of the graves. Tavit told me that a portion of the prayer for the dead was on the stone. The man was a father and grandfather. His name was Muhi Eldan, son of Yusef. His family name was Al Disdar. He was Muslim. On the tombstone it is written that he was a "Guard of the Ottoman Empire." He died in 1913. Tavit, who seems to know everyone, laughed when I asked him to translate the Arabic on the grave. "What's so funny?" I asked. "I know that guy's grandkids," he said. "One became a filmmaker."

The day before I had walked through Mamilla Mall, the outdoor shopping mall full of American retailers like Gap and a few luxury brands such as Rolex. The storefront-lined esplanade seamlessly connects West Jerusalem to East (and has the same name of the cemetery upon which the Museum of Tolerance is being built).

I had just arrived in Jerusalem at dusk, and was meeting Tavit, whom I hadn't seen in years. As I walked through the mall, a clownish figure with a headset and mouthpiece approached me, hopping around like a human pogo-stick. He wore a blue and white sign around his neck that looked like the Israeli flag. His sign said, "No Dividing Jerusalem," with the website address, "United Jerusalem.com." He wore a jacket with the Israeli flag embroidered on one sleeve. I made the mistake of catching his eye as he hopped towards me.

"Don't smile, young lady," he said sarcastically. "Whatever you do, don't smile!" I moved away from him and started walking on the other side of the mall. As a woman, it's infuriating to be told to smile by strange men. I was really excited about seeing Tavit—it had been a long time—but maybe I did look upset. I must have been thinking of other things, too, like that my nostalgia for Jerusalem is a myth, that it isn't just bathed in limestone. "Don't worry," I said back to the man. "I won't."

—Liz Rose Shulman—

"I DIDN'T THINK OF THE PINK LIGHT OR THE STONES AT DUSK"

"Reading a piece of literature that has been translated from Hebrew," Amos Oz said in a 1990 lecture at the University of Wisconsin, "is like making love through a blanket." I swooned. Oz wasn't just talking to me, though it sure felt like it. I was twenty years old, in a lecture hall with 49 other undergrads, taking a Hebrew Literature in Translation course. When Oz spoke, everyone else in the room disappeared. He was good looking—he had intense blue eyes, a lot of gray and sandy brown hair. He was warm, sensitive, sexy, manly. A true Sabra.

Our professor, an Israeli who also chaired the Hebrew and Semitic Studies Department, brought him to speak to our class. Oz talked about the limitations of translation as well as the access it provides. He also discussed his views on the state of contemporary Israeli literature and opened up to us about his own writing process. It was fall semester. Crisp red and brown leaves dotted the campus. Oz mentioned the sound of them under his feet as he walked to our class. Visiting from Israel where he lived, he said, he didn't experience fall like we did in the Midwest.

I grew up reading his books; many of them helped instill my infatuation with Israel. Like the comment to my class, his writing was similarly sexual. He eroticized the land and language of Israel in a way that felt personal and private and it gave me permission to do the same. To meet him up close in a classroom setting was a deep honor. I was an ardent Zionist at the time and I could relate. I hung on Oz's every word.

I stopped hanging on years ago when I began to oppose Zionism, but one year after his death, I've been thinking about the intense ways he influenced my mode—and eventual undoing—of liberal Zionism.

A few weeks after Oz's visit, I sat in the department chair's office asking him about study abroad programs in Israel. I had visited for the first time in high school on the eight-week summer program when I was 16, but I was dying to return, and for a longer period. The Chair wrote me a letter of recommendation to attend Hebrew University of Jerusalem for a master's degree, which I did, once I graduated.

Of course, Oz's comments like the one he made to our class about the constraints of translated literature weren't wrong. You miss out on an authentic experience when you read in translation. The professor of a Nabakov and Dostoevsky course I took at Hebrew University—she had immigrated to Israel decades earlier from Moscow—once told me that nothing in the world compared to reading these two great authors in their original Russian. One afternoon, once I had been living in Israel for a few months, I visited during her office hours. She told me I looked tired, then asked how my Hebrew was coming along. I admitted I felt a constant sort of fatigue living in another country, trying to learn another language. She said my exhaustion would dissipate as my Hebrew improved.

There, in Jerusalem, while I lived my dream, Oz's literature came to life. His prose portrayed an Israel that was mythical and romantic—an Israel I saw with my own eyes. Once I arrived, I saw first-hand the intense love he narrated so beautifully in his books.

I had read many of his books as an undergrad in the 1990s and I remember the quiet, reflective tone. Studying in Wisconsin, I loved Israel from afar; which is to say I romanticized the tiny country long before I lived there. Jerusalem was like a long-distance lover I pined for so that when I moved there in 1992 for graduate school, the Jerusalem I saw was the one presented in Oz's books.

There, in Jerusalem, I saw what Oz saw. My favorite time of day in the city was dusk when the light hit the stone of the city walls like a golden-pink rose. I knew about that light years before I arrived to Israel: I drew it with pink and orange crayons in Hebrew school, sang songs about it at Zionist summer camp, read about it in the JUF newsletter on my parent's kitchen table. It wasn't only Oz's books that helped turn me into a liberal Zionist, of course. The efforts to recruit young Jews into a nationalistic fervor for Zionism has long been manufactured, deliberately outlined by other smarter and older Zionists sitting in large offices with millions of dollars, strategizing how to get people like me to fall in love with the land. They made sure it would feel like a private experience that I could only share with other young Zionists who felt the same. Reading Oz simply solidified this growing love—and he personalized it with fantastic prose.

There, in Jerusalem, as I walked through Jaffa Gate, the morning smells of olives and za'atar and lemon and mint wafted through the corridors of the Old City again and again. The Arab store owners opened the doors of their shops and set their items out for the day as they bargained with tourists. By the end of the afternoon—when the rose light started to hit the stone—the Arab shop owners would start putting away everything that hadn't sold that day. They'd wash the ancient stone in front of their shops and do it all over again the next day.

It strikes me now that, like Oz often did, I too, referred to Palestinians as Arabs. I saw them as exotic background scenery like I had read about in his books—from there, sort of, insofar as they add to the scene but with passivity and a lack of legitimacy.

One could argue, of course, that Oz does give voice to Palestinians in his books. *In the Land of Israel,* for example, is based on conversations Oz had with Palestinians and Israelis throughout the country and he quotes the people he talked to extensively. But the book still has a romanticized, mythical feel to it:

Snow on the graves of the soldiers who died in the war in Lebanon. Snow on the soldiers still fighting in Lebanon to separate the Druses from the Christians in the Shouf Mountains, the Christians from the Palestinians in Tyre and Sidon, to separate curse from curse.

It's a tragic and doomed but beloved land Oz intimates, and all the players seem to know it. Though Oz traveled around the country on "a journey among people of strong convictions," as stated in his book—"individuals inclined to exclamation points"—he still maintained a convenient distance from acknowledging Palestinian history.

Instead, Oz chose when to use the word Arab and when to use Palestinian. He referred to "Arab villages," "Arab laborers," "Arab towns," "the Israeli-Arab conflict," throughout *In the Land of Israel*. He asked a settler, "who is right, the Arabs or us?" Oz enticed readers like me with a seemingly progressive stance. Deeper inside the writing, however, Oz stopped short and unveiled colonialist rhetoric.

But I wasn't thinking about any of that when I was in love with Israel. Like Oz, I stopped short, too. I believed I could be both a lover of justice and a Zionist—these weren't in opposition for me back then. Indeed, Zionism and Judaism were synonymous in my mind, and so, I relished and romanticized Jerusalem like Oz did.

There, in Jerusalem, among the cobblestones of Yoel Solomon Street, was Champs Bar, where I fell in love with Tavit at age twenty-two. Unlike me, Tavit was from there. He showed me different parts of the city—little and big places he knew in East and West Jerusalem as he zig-zagged between both worlds.

There, in Jerusalem, in a quiet corner of the courtyard behind the noises of Yoel Solomon Street in back of the jewelry store Turquoise, Tavit and I fooled around on what I believed were ancient Jewish stones. Even the sounds that snuck over the wall of the courtyard had a calm to them. "[T]hat Jerusalem stillness which can be heard," Oz described in *In the Land of Israel*, "if you listen for it, even in the noisiest street." After, we walked back into Champs, giggling, thinking no one knew what we had been up to.

There, in Jerusalem, in the middle of Zion Square, I met friends in the evenings getting off the buses on Jaffa Road after my grad classes. We exchanged money illegally with the Orthodox guy adjacent to the square who would only do it when his father wasn't lurking in the shop—where we also bought packs of cigarettes, a different brand for each of us as though to assert our various personalities as we smoked.

There, in Jerusalem, on Ben Yehuda Street, several of us girls locked arms and kicked up our legs and danced when we were drunk. Israelis who worked in the restaurants nearby looked at us and scoffed, tired, for they were working for a living while we drank, our extended student-visas tucked into our American passports in our backpacks. We ate at Apple Pizza and made fun of each other for eating the featured corn and pineapple slices.

There, in Jerusalem, on the 23 bus we sang out loud our favorite Zionist songs—"Eli, Eli," "Halleluya," "Yerushalayim shel Zahav," ("Jerusalem of Gold") were just a few—as we rode through Palestinian neighborhoods, ignoring, too, the Palestinians on the bus with us we thought of as Arabs.

There, in Jerusalem, on Jaffa Road near Nahalat Shiva, the bald shop owner sold condoms to Tavit, winking at me as we left the shop to make our way to the corner of the courtyard behind Turquoise. My sexual coming-of-age was inseparable from the ways I sexualized the land. Jerusalem was sex itself (who'd rather have sex on a cold stone than a bed?). I remember reading Oz's 1979 *Under This Blazing Light* in college, where he also sexualized Jerusalem:

> Sometimes, when I had nothing better to do, I used to go to Jerusalem to woo her…Jerusalem is mine, yet a stranger to me; captured and yet resentful; yielding yet withdrawn.

One night, Tavit drove us up a hill and we sat in his car gazing down at the Old City walls with the professed perspective of a wise sage—though it was mostly bravado. Outside it was quiet. We didn't talk. "[O]ne felt an urge to sprawl facing the view of the city walls," Oz wrote in *A Tale of Love and Darkness*, "to doze in the shade of the foliage or calmly drink in the silence of the hills and the stone." Tavit said Jerusalem and I both had sexy, curvy hips as we surveyed the city's hills in between its stones. There, in Jerusalem, he squeezed my hips. I traced the arch of his eyebrow with my finger, comparing it to the arch of those hills, too, as I'd done many times before.

There, in Jerusalem, at the Western Wall, my friends and I smoked a joint, dozing on and off all night on the huge stones that look like benches at the back of the plaza, confident the Israeli police on guard would protect us. They laughed when they smelled our weed. We laughed, too, unaware of the extent of our privilege. They refused when we offered it to them, which, of course, we thought was classy. Then we practiced our paltry Hebrew, asking them to correct us—giving them even more power than they already had.

There, in Jerusalem's Russian Compound, my friends dared me to kiss an Israeli soldier outside of the bar Glasnost next to the bar Cannabis. "Is that your M16 or are you just happy to see me?" I asked, though the idiom was lost because I had garbled a few Hebrew words I knew. I smiled and tossed my head back, drunk from the White Russian drinks I had earlier. The soldier, who had striking green eyes and curly black hair, flirted back. My friends started chanting, "nshika, nshika, nshika"—"kiss, kiss, kiss" in Hebrew—and we began to make out against the bar's stone wall. I felt his M16 against my thigh as he pushed himself against me.

My Hebrew got better with each year I spent in Jerusalem—I would live there five in total before returning here, to Chicago—and I realized my professor had been right. The exhaustion that came with learning another language while living in a foreign country had evaporated.

I often thought about Oz's comment to my class about the limitations of translation. If reading literature translated from Hebrew was like making love through a blanket, as he said, then its opposite was also true. Speaking

Hebrew was sexy and raw and real. It was private and intimate too. It was the language of the land I was in love with.

Of course, Hebrew is also the language of Israel's ongoing military occupation of millions of Palestinians who have been dehumanized in Hebrew, evicted and expelled in Hebrew, the language Palestinians routinely hear at checkpoints. But I wasn't concerned with all that. I was thinking about Oz's passage in *Under This Blazing Light* where he writes that private acts, when done in Hebrew, guarantee you're in the heart of the language:

> If you live in Hebrew, if you think, dream, make love in Hebrew, sing in Hebrew in the shower, tell lies in Hebrew, you are 'inside.'

It's true that one develops an intimacy with language. I remember the first dream I had in Hebrew after studying it for years. I woke up with a new confidence with the language that felt very private to me.

It was necessary for Israel, of course, to create a culture around Hebrew after 1948, a phenomenon Motti Regev and Edwin Seroussi, in their 2004 book, *Popular Music & National Culture in Israel,* call the "nostalgic industry." Through Hebrew songs—the same songs I sang on the 23 bus with my friends—the music became "the central Zionist project of inventing a new, 'native' Jewish national culture in Israel." Like someone who has been pre-programmed, my experience of singing with my friends, while seemingly spontaneous, had already been planned and manufactured by those smarter and older Zionists sitting in their large offices.

In *Under This Blazing Light,* Oz wrote that the revival of the Hebrew language "can indeed be seen as the most certain achievement of Zionism." In the same book, Oz sexualizes Hebrew by comparing it to a woman who teases and taunts:

> The New Hebrew is, so to speak, a flirt in heat. One day she is seemingly all yours and completely with you, at your feet, ready for anything, happy

for any audacious activity, and all at once you're lying there behind her, flat on her back and a trifle ridiculous, and she runs off to her new lovers…

The Hebrew language, like the land itself was flirty, sexual, erotic.

These things were true for me. But other things were true, too, like the way my experiences followed the prescribed, contrived formula to get young Zionists like me to fall in line—while we fell in love—and to have us believe that our experiences were unique and individualized.

Later, in Jerusalem, I could identify cracks in the myth, seeds that were planted along the way, but undoing Zionism was a slow process. In my 30s I began talking with Palestinians and listening to their stories of expulsion and occupation. I started reading Edward Said and Ilan Pappe and Amira Hass and others who had long been writing about Palestine. I visited Palestine and stayed with Palestinians. Once I had undone my Zionism, I saw everything differently.

Later, in Jerusalem, I hung out mostly with Armenians and Palestinians. I didn't have many Jewish friends the farther I moved away from them politically in Israel and the few I did were studying abroad like I was. Something inside me I could not name knew the land wasn't just for the Jews. Despite the messages I received growing up, I must have felt in my core something unsettling. Regardless of its intense beauty, I began to see Oz's prose as limited. He stopped short, whereas I and so many others had gone farther. It's still some of the most beautiful prose I've ever read.

Later, in Jerusalem, I returned, after opposing Zionism. There, on Jaffa Road, I saw the city as a backdrop of a play in which I had been a player: Mamilla Mall seamlessly connecting new stones to ancient ones—attaching West Jerusalem to East—by way of fancy shops. Birthright participants spend a night in a Bedouin tent on Day 8 of 10—a deliberate scheduling maneuver by those smarter and older Zionists sitting in their large offices who count on the sexual tension that has built up during Days 1-8 between the participants. Before the young Zionists fool around later—many of them for the first time while on their first trip to Israel—they're served tea by Bedouins they've been taught to fetishize.

There, in Jerusalem, buses of tourists, young Zionists eager to consummate their love for the land, arrived by the thousands, and are shuffled into fancy hotels. It wasn't quiet. It wasn't calm. I didn't think of the pink light or the stones at dusk.

Now, in Chicago, when I look at Oz's books on my bookshelf, I'm not sure what to do. I reread many of them while writing this essay, and Oz's prose was just as beautiful as I remembered. But it was dripping with the liberal Zionism that I grew up with. His books were hard to read. I had spent decades longing for something that was a myth while Palestinians longed for the land that had been taken from them. Oz just couldn't ever get past his own yearning for the only land he ever loved. "[D]o not cut loose from those longings," Oz wrote on the last page of *In the Land of Israel*, "for what are we without our longings?"

EARLY LOVE STORY:
HOW MANY MORE ORGASMS WILL BE HAD FOR ZIONISM?

Last week I ran into my ex-boyfriend, Mark, at a Whole Foods salad bar. We had dated on and off for about fifteen years, and spent many summers together at summer camp in Three Rivers, Michigan, in the early 1980s. When I saw him reaching for the cottage cheese right next to the tofu I was reaching for, I thought about turning away and not saying anything, pretending that I hadn't seen him. I had a second to decide—he was moving on to the barbecue chicken on the other side—and in that moment a flurry of memories came to mind. I thought, at first, what a horrible way to run into an ex, at a Whole Foods salad bar, and then, I remembered how much I loved him during the high school, college, and graduate school years we were periodically together. My deep love for him was fiercely connected to my deep love for Israel because it had been born at camp. Ultimately, I decided to turn towards him and say hello.

Like many other Jewish American youth, I spent several summers at Jewish camp. I was part of the Habonim (Hebrew for "builders") youth movement, a Zionist-Socialist camp that models itself on a kibbutz. We lived in Israeli tents that we, American suburban Jews, put together ourselves. We sang "Hatikvah" every morning at the flagpole as we raised the Israeli flag. We worked in the morning, we lived in nature, and we developed a sense of who we were and who we wanted to be—living out a particular kind of egalitarian idealism in a simulated kibbutz. We were fashioning a mode of liberation available to us only in the eight-week summer session of camp. During the school year, we were young, mostly upper-middle class, budding suburban capitalists—Jews in a secular world (destined later in life to shop for tofu and organic meats at Whole Foods).

In the evenings at camp, after Israeli folk dancing, we fooled around, exploring our sexuality in a space seemingly filled with freedom and openness, as we deepened our love for Israel at our simulated kibbutz. Our adoration for Israel was a kind of love that, for me and many other young Zionists, felt much like a first love—a deep attachment to something felt strongly in our hearts. The bunk beds in our tents touched each other and only sheer mosquito netting separated us. One night a friend in the bunk next to mine had sex for the first time—our bunk beds so close that the metal bars on my bed were shaking as he and another camper moved on top of each other—and I could hear the Israeli music from the Israeli folk dancing still in the distance. Though I wasn't the one losing my virginity, I felt part of something big.

Jewish American Zionist camps help to develop identity among Jewish youth. They teach important decision-making skills in a supposed democratic collective. They're designed to instill and deepen a love for Israel. They are also a place for young people to learn about living away from home and they become a space to experiment sexually under the nationalistic ethos of Zionism. Most of the camps associated with these Zionist youth movements have a goal to build a love for Israel that might ultimately persuade Jews to move there. Habonim, for example, features a gap year in between high school and college called "Workshop," where high school graduates in a work/study program live on a kibbutz for the year. The Habonim website features a video about "Hannah," a young woman who describes Workshop as a "Labor Zionist youth movement whose main goal is to create social justice and Jewish values in Israeli society." Hannah is spending her Workshop year, she tell us in her video, "teaching about equality and shared existence" in various Arab villages.

Arriving in Israel, and setting foot on the land, finally, for the first time, the Jewish youth consummate the unrequited wandering of the diaspora. The summer camp becomes a kind of foreplay, the anticipation builds for years, and landing in Israel is the ultimate fulfillment. I know the feeling well. A letter I sent to my parents in 1992, when I was a Zionist, two months after arriving in Israel for graduate school reads, "I've finally made it to Israel. And I'll be here long enough to see the seasons change." I also described the Palestinian man I was dating (not telling them he was Palestinian). "I knew I loved him when I saw him look towards the Judean Hills," I wrote, "and I noticed how his chin was aligned perfectly with the hills." The "Judean Hills" are occupied Palestine, of course, and as a Palestinian man, he was looking out at his homeland, Palestine. In sexualizing my experience in Israel—eroticizing the Zionist connection between person and place—I had appropriated his. I didn't know better. The angle of his chin was very attractive to my hormone-flooded self, which was in love, and far from home. I did the same thing with Tavit.

During the camp summer sessions we were Socialists who believed in the motto we chanted, "Give what you can, take what you need." This saying was specifically meant for our additional pot of money, collected separately from our tuition. We called this extra money "Kupah," Hebrew for "cash register." Habonim explains the concept of Kupah on its website:

> [I]n Habonim Dror we translate it as a 'cooperative fund.' Kupah is how we incorporate elements of cooperative living into camp life. All campers pool their funds and then decide as a democratic community how to use those funds. The idea of Kupah is one of the most important elements in the educational program and ideology of Habonim Dror. Through Kupah campers learn about sharing, teamwork, compromise, democracy, budgeting and more. Kupah funds are also used as a central canteen from which campers can draw small personal necessities such as toiletries, stationery, etc. The fund can also be used for special treats as decided by the campers.

It was our parents, of course, who paid for all of our camp expenses. One summer, a camper's Kupah check for twenty-five dollars was found crumpled, torn, and unreadable by the lake (today, Kupah costs $120 per camper for the summer session). The camper called her dad and he promptly sent another check. We found it silly at the time, unaware of our privilege to be able to be so nonchalant about money. Sure, we made fun of the recklessness in which funds were handled, wondering—but not for too long—how did the check become crumpled, torn, ending up by the lake in the first place? We could laugh about it because we knew that such a mistake as a lost check could be easily replaced. There would always be enough in Kupah.

In our minds, overnight camp became a playground where we got to leave our homes and create a new kind of family. We sat in circles, held group discussions, and talked through problems as they came up. We communicated better at camp than most of us did at home. We expressed ourselves in ways we couldn't with our families. We were creating a new way to be—not unlike a Sabra—shedding our old selves for a few thousand dollars each summer. Creating our new identities at camp extended to our Zionism as well. Like the Zionists who immigrated to Israel to "settle the land" and "make the desert bloom," thereby shedding their old American and European selves, we too, were developing a new way of being, leaving behind our old ways at home, three hours away down Interstate 90.

My ex-boyfriend Mark would tell me years later when we attended a camp friend's wedding together, that he was one of the two people who lost his virginity that night in the bunk bed. This was not uncommon. Many people at camp had their first sexual experiences in these Israeli-made tents in the woods or in the bathrooms where we took naked group baths together. Afternoon "educational" sessions on Shabbat included girls sitting in a circle chanting, "I am a woman and I have a vagina." It felt weird to do this, of course, but it followed discussions about sex and womanhood that I hadn't experienced before. We read and discussed the groundbreaking book, *Our Bodies, Ourselves,* like it was scripture. The book, published in 1971, revealed things to us that we had wondered about privately but had never talked about with others. I had been very shy at home, and learning about my body in a kibbutz-style collective felt different and open. We were young, attractive teenagers who were given permission to experiment and talk about our bodies. We skinny-dipped at night, scrubbed bathrooms in the morning, cooked, cleaned, and believed that we were working for something much greater and bigger than ourselves.

One day we decorated a large map of Israel with ice cream, frosting, and other toppings. The forests—many years later I'd understand these were Palestinian villages ethnically cleansed and replaced with pine trees—were decorated with green frosting. The desert, soon to be populated with olim, like us, was caramel. The rivers and sea, a blue ice cream called, at the time, Smurf. The whipped cream was a bonus. We then ate the whole thing—all the bright colors melting together across the Golan Heights like a sad, crazy clown face, zigzagging down the Jordan River, dripping above Jerusalem. It was a distorted rainbow, and we—licking Israel at the same time licking our fingers—wondered who would hook up that night. We were digging into the land with our hands and our hearts while thinking about sex. We believed in Israel's Socialist Zionism and played out the role perfectly in a large plot of land near a lake. If we could feel so good about ourselves at camp during the summer, the idea was, we could attend Workshop and feel this way for a year, or ultimately, we could make aliyah, live on a kibbutz, and feel this way forever.

Although by a young age I had already developed a nationalism born of the fusion of sexuality and Zionism, my story preceded the emergence of Birthright trips. It followed, all the same, the manufactured convergence of sexuality and Zionism that has grown into what is now Birthright. Much has been written about the forced sexuality that occurs on these trips which are designed to recreate the summer camp feel, this time consummated in Israel. For example, Rose Surnow's essay, "I Gave a Handy at Jew Camp," details her Birthright trip, calling it an "all-expenses-paid orgy in the desert," describing a Bedouin tent in the West Bank where "45 of us were going to sleep in one massive tent in the desert, which in our sleazy minds meant HOOK-UP-CITY." Like Surnow and others have written, my deepened love for Israel was inextricable from my sexual coming of age. The boundaries and sense of place and person—of body and nation—merged seamlessly. Like the hypersexualized experiences of youths at U.S. Jewish summer camps, Birthright participants also find themselves in situations where sexual experiences are encouraged. Some websites even offer advice on such sexual matters for Birthright participants such as, "The Unofficial Guide to Sex and Drugs on Birthright Trips," in which potential hookups are encouraged. This website gives advice on condom usage as well as rules for "hooking up" with soldiers, counselors, and other participants.

One night at camp, we sat around a campfire singing Bob Marley and David Bowie songs. In between singing, we were quiet, listening to the crickets around us, mesmerized by the crackling of the campfire, the popping of red and orange underneath the burning wood. It smelled like sandalwood and felt cozy and new. Someone played the guitar softly. Back at home my father had joked that "Jews don't camp," and the closest that we'd ever get to camping would be to stay in a cheap hotel. Here at camp, I was outside all the time. I would miss those nights as I got older.

This particular night during our campfire we discussed whether or not we were going to take the gap year and go to Israel for Workshop. I sat with Mark. He confided in me later that night, as we were lying in his bunk bed—the mosquito netting our canopy—that instead of going to Israel for Workshop he thought he might want to study in Korea or Japan. He was becoming more interested in Asian cultures. He thought that as a group we were becoming too "Israeli-centric"—that was the point, of course, of being a part of Habonim—and that it was important to study other places too. He thought that I should as well and often criticized my unconditional love of Israel over the years we were together.

As young Zionists who finally made it to Israel sometime after our years of camp (for me, it was the mid-1990s), we knew we weren't the first to have a sexual connection to the land, but somehow when we did for the first time, we felt like the only ones who ever had. We were simply recreating the Zionist ethos we had been a part of at camp, feeling nostalgia for our childhood and our budding sexuality. It is a brilliant brainwashing tactic—like Pinkwashing—to build our nationalistic Zionist love for a land that continues to occupy and expel Palestinians. In all my years at camp, I never once heard the word Palestine and I didn't learn about Palestinians. Despite these evasions—this is why it is difficult to write about—my years at camp were some of the best of my life. I learned so much about myself in those summers. I felt an openness and freedom that is often available only to youth. Some of my closest and oldest friendships are still with people I met at camp. Last week as I was working on this essay, one of my current students told me she couldn't wait to go back to Habonim this summer. I asked her what it was about the camp that she loved so much. "It's hard to explain," she said. "I just feel like people accept me more there than anywhere else." Her enthusiasm about camp is moving; I remember having the same feelings.

The sexualizing of Zionism—at camp and in Palestine—continues of course. My experience was 32 years ago, but camps like Habonim continue these efforts today. Young campers like my current student will keep going to camp because of how good they feel about themselves when they are there. Like me, she'll grow up and be grateful for the experience—which inevitably involves an eroticized relationship with the land. How many more orgasms will be had for Zionism? How many more ice-cream maps of Israel will be created and then eaten and destroyed at the whim of the colonizer? How many more youths will be lured into the Bedouin tent—empty of Bedouins except for the ones who, desperate for work, serve the Jews tea while they continue to be displaced—to play out an Orientalist, colonialist sex game?

When I saw Mark at the salad bar last week, I remembered how critical he was of me about Israel, and I thought about one of our "off" periods, when I moved to Jerusalem for graduate school. He made it to Japan for the year. I cared at the time far too much what he thought about me. I was worried what traveling to different countries would do to our on-again off-again relationship, that I wasn't radical enough for him, that my life had gone too much the route of a typical Jewish American Zionist. Last week, at the salad bar, he told me that he had gotten married "to a super Jew," a woman who used to do fundraising for the Jewish Federation. They had three kids. Their son had recently had his Bar-Mitzvah in Jerusalem. He was excited—I should have known this was coming—to someday send his kids to camp. He must have heard about my Israel/Palestine activism work, because he asked, with a small smirk on his face if I was still "marching in the streets, waving flags of

Palestine." We walked out of the supermarket together, holding our salads, and moved towards the parking lot. I didn't watch to see which way he went.

O Jerusalem, Please Forget Me

It's 25 years since I was a student at Hebrew University and I've just arrived to do some research on how West Jerusalem has changed. I've come with my husband, Tony, who has never been here. He'll be with me for a week and then I'll stay another week on my own to work. My last two visits here were organized as Palestinian solidarity trips all over the West Bank; I haven't seen West Jerusalem in years. A friend tells me I must show my husband Tel-Aviv and West Jerusalem as I research the changes, "so he can see the apartheid society they have made for themselves."

We spend one day in Tel-Aviv before heading to Jerusalem. Our driver, Eldad, (a friend insisted that his friend's friend drive us) is excited that it is Tony's first time here. Eldad takes Road 443 because "it will be much faster than Highway 1." When we get into his car, I see several Israeli flags on the dashboard, and I anticipate his reaction when he asks specifically where we are going in Jerusalem. I tell him the name and address of the hotel we're staying at in East Jerusalem. He looks at me strangely and asks, "You said you used to live here?"

I've never been on Road 443 before, and he narrates as we make the slow climb up to Jerusalem. It doesn't feel like much of an ascent and I wonder if I've misremembered the steep climb I used to feel when going up to

Jerusalem. Later I learn that Road 443 runs more smoothly along the ridge line, whereas Highway 1 goes up and down through mountains and valleys and is a much more dramatic ascent. As we make our way on 443 Eldad points to Givat Zeev on our right. He explains to Tony that the "city" has grown tremendously. Tony knows it's a settlement, but neither of us say anything. Ramallah is on our left, and we see Ofer prison. "Israel takes very good care of its prisoners," Eldad says. "The prison was built close, so the families can easily visit the terrorists. Nowhere else in the world are terrorists treated so well." For a few minutes, we see the wall Israel has built, cutting Palestinians off from their own land. Eldad explains that there have been hardly any attacks since the wall was built. "It's much safer now," he says, looking at Tony in the rear view mirror. We pass seamlessly through the checkpoint. We've come at Jerusalem from behind and it's too fast. I'll tell Tony this later, and he'll tease me, telling me that I needed more foreplay with Jerusalem. It's true. I was expecting a slow entry and now I'm trying to get my bearings as we enter quickly. I see the sign for Pisgat Zeev. Later, I'll see signs for Maale Adumim. I've noticed a change in signage here. The signs for the settlements appear to me more seamlessly a part of Jerusalem's geography, as though they've always been a part of the city. Finally I recognize the road towards Mt. Scopus. Now I know where we are. When we arrive to the hotel, Eldad shakes our hands after we pay him. He looks at me like a concerned father to his daughter. "Be safe," he says.

Later, we walk to Kikar Zion in West Jerusalem. I can't find Jaffa Road. A few minutes later I realize that we're standing on it as the tram goes by and young yeshiva girls walk in the middle of the street. I'm embarrassed that I don't recognize things. I had promised Tony I'd be an excellent tour guide. "Are you sure you know the city?" he asked me weeks before the trip. "It's been a long time since you were there." "Of course!" I replied. "I remember Jerusalem like the back of my hand. I haven't forgotten." Now he has to wait for me to get my bearings; he has no point of reference. I remember Jaffa Road as an actual road with sidewalks and cars and buses. It's become a pedestrian mall like so much of the downtown. I don't recognize it. Tony doesn't quite understand my meltdown. "All cities change," he says. "It's not just that," I try to explain. "Jerusalem is different," I say, even though I know that sounds like Jewish exceptionalism. The change of the physical geography of the land has caused an internal change in the mind. The result is a colonization of the hearts and minds of Zionists everywhere and manifests itself with the new landscape appearing ancient and permanent. This is not the West Jerusalem I recall in my mind. But the one I remember had been colonized as well, and I know now that my memory of what I remember as the "original" was also a manufactured colonization of Palestine, 1990s style.

We walk through Mamilla Mall towards Jaffa Gate. It's a beautiful outdoor pedestrian mall with fancy shops next to "ancient ruins." Mamilla was the name of the neighborhood in Jerusalem founded in the late 19th century just outside the Old City near the Jaffa Gate. As I've walked through hotel lobbies in West Jerusalem the last few days, the phrase I've heard repeated over and over at the concierge desk is American Jews asking, "How do you get to Mamilla Mall?" The mall has seamlessly connected West Jerusalem to the Old City at Jaffa Gate with loads of shops.

Later I read about how Mamilla Mall was reported in the Israeli news. Aviva and Shmuel Bar-Am's article from *The Times of Israel* ("Mamilla, the Jerusalem border neighborhood that rose from the rubble," November 21, 2015,) celebrates the new mall—perpetuating the myth that Israel has once again restored something that had been destroyed by its enemies. Mamilla is "an incredible story of destruction, division, unification, renewal—and now shopping," the article states, and it "begins at Jaffa Gate a century ago." The article emphasizes that West Jerusalem was always connected to the Old City, and justifies the "rebuilding." "Mamilla was a tiny neighborhood located on the seam that connects Old and New Jerusalem," the article says. "In the early 1900s, dozens of shops, consulates, banks and guesthouses completely covered the area from just outside the gate to today's IDF Square." The article tells the "story" of the "incensed" Arabs after they learned that "the United Nations approved a plan to create a Jewish state in Palestine. The country's Arabs swore "to prevent its formation with the last drop of their blood." The Arabs screamed "slogans and armed with knives and iron bars, they began looting and ransacking Jewish shops. Then they set them on fire." The article also states that plans for "restoring" the mall began in 1967:

After the reunification of Jerusalem in 1967, and the eye-sore that was No-Man's Land was removed, plans began to form for rehabilitation of the ravaged Mamilla neighborhood…Decades of conflict between architects and planners ended when the first stage of the Alrov Mamilla Avenue opened in 2007. An open-air mall, it was designed by architect Moshe Safdie, and developed by the Alrov Group.

The article also mentions some of the buildings in Mamilla Mall that date back to 1870 and 1886. "From sing-alongs to an open museum on Independence Day, Mamilla hosts all kinds of events," the article concludes, "An all-around smashing success, Mamilla Mall unites Old and New Jerusalem—just as it did in the past." Mamilla Mall seems like the most brilliant form of colonization and apartheid. The wall that separates Palestinians from access to their land and keeps them from their loved ones is a dehumanizing daily reminder of their restricted life under occupation. For the Israelis and others visiting Jerusalem, apartheid is the Gap, North Face, American Eagle, Clarks, Timberland, Nine West, spaghetti, steak, and pizza restaurants, and, of course, the jewelry store Padani—"Jewelry for Connoisseurs"—all of which connect the West to the East and keep the shoppers busy.

Shabbat morning, a few days after Tony returns to the U.S., I walk down Jaffa Road towards the Old City to visit Tavit, who still lives in the Armenian Quarter. Orthodox families walk in the street. A little boy walks along the train tracks. A few homeless people sleep on benches, the smells of urine and feces waft around them. I meet Tavit and we drink coffee. Then we walk and he shows me the house he bought in the Old City that is on the border of the Armenian and Jewish Quarters. I'm happy for him. I joke and remind him that when we dated 25 years ago, I never saw his home. He was always at my apartment. He never told his parents about us because they wanted him to marry an Armenian. I've recently read some of the letters from him when we were together. "Thank you for making me a home in Jerusalem," he wrote. He doesn't remember this when I tell him. I confess to him that I used to walk by his parents' house on Armenian Patriarch Road whenever I was in the Old City. I'd see the red and pink roses that he'd planted for his parents, and over time I watched the way that they grew out over the wall of their house. Now, we drink tea in his living room. His wife and kids are in Lebanon for a few weeks visiting his wife's family. He married an Armenian, he tells me. He's recently planted rose bushes in his garden. There's a lemon tree too. I tell him I married a Buddhist, show him pictures of Tony and me in Jerusalem a few days ago, and he laughs, knowing it was unlikely that I'd marry a Jew. He says he wishes he could have met Tony. It's quiet in his house. There's a wonderful breeze coming in through the window. I remember our time together 25 years ago. Looking at our lives now, I can hardly imagine that our paths crossed so intimately. It seems unlikely now that they ever would have. They certainly wouldn't in today's Jerusalem. The bar we met at, full of secular ex-pats and internationals, closed down 20 years ago.

After a little while, Tavit talks about his shop on Salah Al-Din Street in East Jerusalem and the work he does in West Jerusalem. I've always loved his perspective on Jerusalem. He lives in both worlds of East and West. He became my bridge of East and West when I was living here. He showed me places in East Jerusalem, took me to Ramallah and Bethlehem, and then slept over in my apartment in West Jerusalem. I ask him about Mamilla Mall. He says that his great-grandfather used to live in the Mamilla area alongside Palestinians. His great-grandfather had his first shop there. He's sick of Jerusalem, he says. "The Muslims are becoming more Muslim, and the Jews are becoming more Jewish," he tells me as he rolls his cigarette.

Walking back from Tavit's house in the Old City later Saturday afternoon, I decide to walk through Mamilla Mall again. An old man plays Sinatra's "New York, New York" on the saxophone. A small group of American Jewish college students lock arms and kick their legs up in rhythm as he plays. They're loud and unselfconscious. They look like they might have been up all night. I think I must have looked and behaved like they are now when I lived here as a student 25 years ago, but I can't remember.

As I exit the mall, I look back at the Old City walls. It's late afternoon and the light is hitting the stone. This I remember. But it's a colder kind of light now. I used to stare at the warm golden rock at this time of day when I lived here and I'd think of Psalm 137:5, "If I forget thee, O Jerusalem, let my right hand forget her cunning." I would never forget. But I have forgotten so much. And now I think Jerusalem wants me to forget her. "Please forget me," I think she is saying. Or it's in my mind. I'm not sure.

Her walls look tired. The people inside her walls look tired and frustrated. She has been forced to change too much by those taking advantage of her, entering her from all sides, changing how she looks, and leaving nothing for those who were here first. The palm trees sway in the wind and look tired too. I have to admit to myself that my own mind has been colonized as well. I realize my folly. I wanted to show my husband a place that doesn't exist, and I've realized it only after he's returned to the U.S. My memories were bigger than the truth. Even though I am an anti-Zionist, I have done the very thing that I have criticized Zionists for doing, believing the Israel of my imagination over its reality.

I'll share this with Tony when I come back to our home. I want to believe that the purest, truest sense of home is only in our minds, created with our loved ones and not in a physical place. But Israel and Palestine is all about place: open-air prisons, apartheid walls, restricted access, advertisements for the privileged reminding them that they are "home," and life under occupation, reminding Palestinians that this is not their home. And the things that I think I remember, like light and stones and love and roses, exist only somewhere in the back of my memory, like an old friend who I visit from time to time, and each instance has aged and weathered. Only if I'm lucky will those I share memories with, like Tavit, have their own distorted memory of our time and place together.

When I'm on Jaffa Road once again, after exiting Mamilla Mall and walking a bit, a young man approaches me. He's holding a map of Jerusalem. He's wearing a white t-shirt with red and green writing that says, "There is no such thing as Palestine." It's his first time to Israel, he says. What he sees now will become truth for him, as true as the writing on his t-shirt. I feel like I'm in a haze. He asks me if he keeps walking straight through Mamilla Mall, will he end up at Jaffa Gate? "You sure will," I say.

GOOD JEWISH BOYS AND GIRLS: MY FIRST PORNO

I didn't know Mark was bringing a porno videocassette to the hotel room. I really didn't. It wouldn't have mattered though if I did because I still would have rented the room with him, Lynn, and Jason. I had a crush on Mark and was excited he'd be there. Lynn and Jason knew I liked him too. Even Mark knew. I'm not sure whether this became more or less apparent as the night went on, the four of us teenagers just hanging out in the very average Holiday Inn hotel room with two double beds just west of I-94 on Touhy Avenue in Skokie, Illinois. Mark said his mother was out for the evening, that she wouldn't notice he had taken the porno from her stash. Jason brought an extra VCR from his mom's house in a brown shopping bag. While the two of them hooked it up to the TV, Lynn and I walked down the gray and maroon hall to the vending machine and bought a bag of peanut M&Ms in anticipation of something we didn't quite know.

It was 1987 and we were eleventh graders attending different high schools along Chicago's North Shore, and though we consequently didn't see each other every day at the same school, we were strongly connected by the overnight summer camp we all went to. Living in tents that we assembled together ourselves, we slept in narrow, less than single-sized bunk beds, each with various grades of mosquito netting our parents bought for us before camp started and which we tied to the corners of the beds delicately like we would fasten bows on dresses. Away from home all summer, we developed a sense of who we were and who we wanted to be—living in this simulated kibbutz on 68 acres nestled between Chicago and Detroit. During the academic year, we trudged through our school days with mild depression, Jews in a cold secular, Christian world, longing for the selves we were growing into and nurturing at camp. During the camp summer sessions we were Socialists fulfilling the camp's mission to "empower the youth to dream of and build a more just and peaceful world," though I'm not sure we did make the world a better place.

Some of us did more with each other sexually than others. A friend lost her virginity to another camper behind a shed near the woods. "He lit candles," she whispered to me the next morning. "It was very romantic, though it was such a fire hazard," she joked. We all possessed an air of detachment that revealed our insulation in our upper-middle-class world. We were incapable, I thought back then, of worrying that anything too bad actually would actually happen to any of us; though, of course, this wasn't true. We were simply sheathed in the bubble of camp that also extended beyond its physical edges. When we went into town, for example—a rare endeavor that occurred maybe once a summer—we made fun of the "townies," the Christian locals who had heard, we were sure, of the crazy Jews who stayed at their commune each summer. One Sunday morning we went to Denny's for an all-you-can-eat buffet, lying about our age to the manager, claiming we were younger than we were so we could get the kid price. While Lynn and I slouched our shoulders and curved our backs trying to make ourselves shorter, another camper played footsie with me under the booth while we ate scrambled eggs and pancakes drizzled with too much maple syrup. But despite all the sexual exploits that occurred at camp, I remained fairly innocent. A guy kicked me out of his bed one night when I wouldn't do anything more than kiss him awkwardly.

It was fall when the four of us rented the hotel room. Jason picked up Lynn in his sister's understated, white Toyota Corolla and then me. Mark drove alone in his mom's black Camaro, a sporty two-door with a gold eagle on the hood. Arriving in cars that didn't belong to us, though suited us nonetheless, might have reminded one of the opening and closing scenes of *The Breakfast Club,* the 1985 John Hughes movie—filmed in two different high schools in Chicago's north suburbs, a fact we took enormous pride in given we were tenth graders when the film came out. We had watched it together dozens of times, memorizing lines as banter when we teased each other. Four of the teenagers' stereotyped personalities match the cars their parents drive. Claire, the spoiled rich girl, is in a BMW; Andrew, the athlete, in a pickup truck with the license plate OHIOST, as if he were already headed to Ohio State on a sports scholarship; Brian, the nerd, in a nondescript sedan with his Einstein-homage license plate EMC 2; and Allison, the basket-case, in an old Cadillac. Only John, the burnout, walks across the school field alone, lacking the family structure the others have, and that we had, too—parents who will drive them to and from their Saturday detention at school in their cars. We were unaware of the contradiction we projected onto the world, at once aspiring to a Socialist-based collective yet also admiring the teens in the film who lived a life of privilege, products of their families' capitalist backgrounds.

    With his mother's porn in his Jansport backpack next to him on the passenger seat of his mother's car, Mark turned into the parking lot of the hotel that night from Touhy Avenue with the confidence of the car being his own, bought and paid for with his own hard-earned money, blasting The Clash, the tires screeching beneath him as he pulled into a spot.

    VCRs were still new then, and porn was widely available for the first time for watching at home. In our case, the convenience of porn videocassettes and VCRs on which to view them allowed the four of us teens to see it together at the hotel. I'm unable to recall, however, why we didn't simply watch it at one of our homes, for it seemed we were always hanging out together when our parents were gone for the evening, playing house using the glasses, plates, and cutlery our parents bought, jumping on furniture they had picked out, rough-housing on their rugs, drinking their alcohol. We emulated their lifestyles while claiming to rebel against how they lived, too, while we waited for our own turn at adulthood. We lacked any real sense of the disappointments that would accompany us once we did inhabit the adult world.

Like the grownups in the comic strip "Peanuts" who are left out of the children's world, our parents seemed in the background of our lives too. In a 1975 interview, "Peanuts" creator Charles Schulz said he developed a cast of off-stage adults who are talked about but never seen or heard and emphasized that adults were not needed in his comic strip. Schulz said that once his own children became adults he found out they had been doing things around the house he hadn't imagined. Children have to keep things from their parents, Schulz explained, especially if you've left for the evening. With our parents out, we acted as though our homes were our own, which of course they were, because we belonged to our parents, but we moved in our bodies and around our houses without an awareness. I think now of how hard our parents were working behind the scenes of our youth to pay for their homes. Perhaps the decision to rent the hotel room that night to watch the porno was a way to begin to individuate from our families during the school year as we were doing for eight weeks each year at summer camp (though our parents paid for our camp tuition while we pretended to be Socialists), to experience something new about ourselves outside the home.

The energy in the hotel room that evening before we watched the porno was exciting, perhaps a bit titillating, if we could have even named it that—an awkward mode of platonic foreplay, anticipating the pornography we were going to collectively view in the neutral hotel space a few miles from our homes. But we were also innocent and young, shy yet curious. That we even called it "porno" and not "porn" was perhaps a way to make the adventure more playful, as though adding the "o" to "porn" somehow made the difference between real perverts and us (though the term "porno" does refer exclusively to video, whereas "porn" often is used for all pornographic content). I don't think any of us had had sex yet. And so I believe we were also scared. Once Mark and Jason successfully hooked up the VCR to the hotel TV they suggested we get stoned. They had brought weed, likely also stolen from their parents. After smoking, we quickly got the munchies. Our hunger took precedence over the impending sexual awakening and we soon left the hotel to go to Jack's, a 24-hour greasy diner just across the street. I don't remember what Jason and Mark ordered, but Lynn got a tuna melt on rye, and I had grilled cheese with cheddar and swiss and a chocolate shake, the kind where they give you the extra in a metal cup.

This was decades before the days of the internet, Pornhub, and "porn literacy," as it's now called—the effort to educate teens about porn in safe and trusting places so they don't have unrealistic expectations about relationships and sex. Most teens today look to porn for their sexual education. Porn literacy wasn't needed for teens like us in the 1980s. We simply didn't have the immediate access to it young people have today. Video pornography was almost beyond our reach, forbidden, something teens strategized to steal from their parents who watched it, which was why it was such a big deal that the four of us were going to watch it together at the hotel.

The porno Mark brought had just come out in 1987 and was called *Little Shop of Whores*, a pun off the 1986 film, *Little Shop of Horrors*. I remember how much I loved the wordplay when I saw the title on the videocassette (my love of language led me to major in English in college and earn a Master's Degree in English too). The nerdy attraction I had developed for witty double entendres expanded to include more titles of pornos I found amusing (but had not watched): *You've Got Male, Urban Cowgirls, Ocean's 11 Inches, ET: The Extra Testicle, Night of the Giving Head, The Sperminator, Edward Penishands, Good Will Humping, A Few Hard Men, Village of the Rammed, Breast Side Story, Saturday Night Beaver, A Clockwork Orgy, Any Officer and a Genitalman, Gulp Fiction, Beverly Hills, 9021-ho!, The Bare Bitch Project, My Bare Lady, Buffy the Vampire Layer, Pulp Friction, A Beautiful Behind, Gangbangs of New York, School of Cock, Throbin Hood, On Golden Blonde, Sisterhood of the Traveling Sluts, Romancing The Bone, Brassiere to Eternity*.

Of course, a clever title was never a sure indication that a good film was to follow. In the hotel room, I lay next to Lynn in anticipation on one of the two double beds. Jason and Mark sat on either side of us cross-legged and eager, closer to the TV. Our stuff was on the other bed. Like kids about to watch a rated-G movie with their family, Lynn and I were each on our stomach, our heads propped up by our hands cupping our chins, swinging our knees and feet as we ate the peanut M&Ms, ready for the show.

It wasn't the first time the four of us hung out in a bed together. Months before we were at Lynn's house in Evanston one Saturday night when her parents were seeing a show at a theatre in downtown Chicago. My dad dropped me off at Lynn's and Mark and Jason came later. We were in the guest room on the dormered third floor. The house was huge, modern, beautiful, and a block from Lake Michigan. In the living room was a life-size horse made of stone. The kitchen had just been updated with tiles Lynn's mother brought back from a trip to Israel. The back of the house, a two-story family room, was all glass. The sheets, pillows, and comforter in Lynn's guest bed were fluffy and light. You felt like you were inside of a cloud or a buttery biscuit in that bed, nothing like the sheets and blankets in my house. Buried under the covers with our clothes on, we four pretended to watch TV as we tickled each other. Soon, we removed our socks. My crush on Mark had been growing, so my efforts to tickle and touch him were more pronounced than for Lynn and Jason. Apparently at one point during our evening playing in the guest bed, Jason thought he was holding Lynn's hand, and Mark thought he was holding mine. I happened to lift my head and looked at their arms, and I saw that in fact Jason and Mark were not holding either of our hands but each other's, their fingers intertwined like lovers. I felt a bit encouraged by the thought that Mark had seemingly been reaching for my hand, a brief yet bold move, given our inexperience about sex. "Jason and Mark are holding hands!" I blurted out awkwardly, laughing and pulling back the thick comforter. They seemed surprised, for clearly they had not realized they were touching each other. They quickly let go with a self-conscious laugh, embarrassed, for their pursuit of us had fallen flat. With nervous laughter, we decided to go downstairs to order a pizza, our bare feet slapping the polished oak wood floors on each step like children running on cement at a local pool in the summer.

Another time, we hung out at Mark's mom's house in Wilmette when his mom was gone for the evening. We were jumping up and down on her bed, fully clothed. At one point Mark asked me to have armpit sex—revealing a bit of chivalry, asking for consent for armpit sex!—with him. I nodded, a young girl eager to do anything for her crush, and he soon rammed his armpit into mine as we jumped higher on the bed. I quickly caught on and pushed back. It was hard to feel much of anything, though, our armpits pushing against each other through our thick winter sweaters. His mother had a copy of the 1972 book, *The Joy of Sex,* on her nightstand that shook up and down as we jumped on the bed. We had looked at it together earlier that evening, in distanced awe of the pictures and positions that seemed so far away from us, as though an invisible line of our youth kept us from going further that night. Unbeknownst to us, I realize now, we were naïvely awaiting the adulthood that we thought would go hand in hand with adult sex in big adult king-sized beds, in big houses in the suburbs that adults buy with the adult jobs we'd each have someday.

The Joy of Sex wasn't the only book we marveled at together. At camp, we read and discussed the groundbreaking 1971 book, *Our Bodies, Ourselves,* like it was scripture. The book revealed things to us that we had wondered about privately but had never talked about with others. I had been very shy at home, and learning about the body in a kibbutz-style collective felt different and open. We were young, attractive teenagers who were given permission to experiment and talk about our bodies, and we retained an authority over how far we would or would not go, growing in ways we didn't yet understand. We skinny-dipped at night like little kids who were expanding into adult bodies yet weren't aware, dipping in and out of spaces that were at once erotic and youthful. We scrubbed bathrooms in the morning taking pride in our physical labor, cooked, cleaned, and believed that we were working for something much greater and bigger than ourselves. One night at camp we sat around a bonfire singing David Bowie's 1971 song, "Changes"—these lines are also the epigraph in the opening moments of *The Breakfast Club* (after a few seconds on the screen the words crack to the sound of smashing glass)—confident in Bowie's assertion that we retained agency over who we were in the adult world.

In between singing, we were quiet, listening to the crickets around us, mesmerized by the crackling of the campfire, the popping and crackling of red and orange underneath the burning twigs and branches. It smelled like sandalwood. We wanted the night to last forever though none of us said so, for we were youthfully unaware that such moments like this would become the past. Several of us at camp fantasized about moving to Israel once we graduated from high school to volunteer on a kibbutz, working in the fields picking tomatoes and tilling the land, making our simulated kibbutz camp in Michigan into a longer, extended Socialist reality in the Middle East. Lynn's parents and mine balked and told us no when we asked them if we could defer university for a year. Nowadays, many who can afford it take a gap year in between high school and college, working and volunteering and interning, but it wasn't a branded popular thing that people do when we were younger. We were going to college, our parents insisted, which we both did. We scoffed at them, but ultimately, we did what they said, feigning our supposed independence with bravado.

  Despite most of my memories of hanging out at each other's homes when our parents weren't there, I still felt I knew Lynn, Jason, and Mark's parents much better than any of the parents of friends I'd meet later. Lynn's father read *The New York Times* every morning at breakfast before he went to work, sections of the paper strewn all over the table. Most evenings he brought a fresh baguette home for dinner. Her mom always had fancy sweets in cardboard boxes tied with string from bakeries in downtown Chicago I'd never heard of. Jason's parents got high. One time when Jason and I were smoking a joint in his kitchen, his mother came home and I ran out the back door, scared. "It's fine," he said, coming after me. "She wants some too." Mark's mother was completing her Ph.D. and working full time after her divorce. Once we went to college and met new friends we'd talk about our parents as though they were these odd roommates we were forced to live with when we were younger, a period of our life we had outgrown. Looking back now it's clear that even though we spent so much time at each other's houses with our parents in the background, we were also growing, unknown to ourselves, in ways that would ultimately emulate them—their personalities, mannerisms, belief systems, and modes of being seeping daily deep into our unconscious minds. I wouldn't understand this until I was older, when I would use culturally popular words like "unpack" and "trigger" and "family of origin" to try to understand myself better.

  I remained connected to Lynn, Jason, and Mark's families. Once I graduated from college and was looking for work, Mark's mom hired me to proofread her dissertation. In the 1990s when I was living in Jerusalem as a graduate student, she brought Mark's sister for a visit. I introduced them to a tour guide I knew to show them around the city and hung out with them in and out of their hotel room in between their tours. Lynn's father was the first of our parents to pass away. At the funeral in 2012, Mark showed up and sat next to me, though I hadn't seen him in at least a decade. We were 42 years old, married, no longer in touch. The seats at the synagogue were narrow; we sat close. It was awkward and distant, yet also oddly comforting to sit with someone who knew me when I was young. These days, I've noticed that I have fewer people in my life who are witnesses to my youth like these friends were. Jason was the first of us to get married and the first to get divorced. When his older brother died tragically in an accident in 2016 at age 51, I spent time with Jason at his mom's house in Lincolnwood and got high with them like we used to once in a while. In her grief, stoned, his mother methodically reached for one Reese's peanut butter cup after another from a bag in her freezer.

    I know such moments in our lives don't last forever, but it's also astonishing, I think sometimes, how we've drifted apart. The last time I saw Mark was at Jason's brother's funeral. We hugged and said hello, shared in the shock that Jason's brother had died so young. We haven't spoken since.

    Little Shop of Whores was unimpressive. I don't remember much except for the opening scene. The camera focuses on a woman's face while she paints her nails, chews and snaps her gum loudly, and talks on the phone, seemingly bored. It occurred to me later that she was in a similar position as I was on the bed, laying on her stomach, her hand cupping her chin. When the camera zoomed out, though, we could see that a man was having sex with her from behind while she showed her detached annoyance. After so much buildup I was let down by watching someone so uninterested in sex engaging in it on the screen in front of us. It wasn't erotic. It wasn't romantic. It was boring. I gave Lynn a look that said, "That's it?" with no words to describe the anticlimactic nature that night became. Despite all the anticipation and imagining we had put into what that night could be like—even though we really had no idea what it might have been when the night began—we were disappointed.

I wonder now if back then I had a feeling that our evening together would be meaningful for me as I got older—if I would look back on that night with nostalgia, for nothing like it would happen again. And though I was unable to express the disappointment, I knew I felt a sadness, perhaps, a hint of what was to come later when I actually did become an adult and had other experiences over the decades with other people in other beds, some who would care for me deeply and some who would not at all, and I wonder if these moments that make up a life mean more or less to me as they tuck themselves into the folds of the back of my brain and become memory as I age. I remember a discussion in English class about the end of *Romeo and Juliet* when I was a freshman in high school, two years before Lynn, Jason, Mark and I would watch the porno. Our teacher asked us if we believed love could last forever, and most of the class said no, based on the tragic death of the two young lovers. "Is love any less meaningful," she pushed, sitting on top of a desk at the front of the classroom, "if it doesn't last forever?" I remember feeling my heart racing. I wanted an answer. I've never forgotten that discussion, not only because I was a teenager who would soon begin to experience losses in love, but because I would return to that question myself many times as an adult. But I've still come up short trying to figure it out. I simply don't know.

We didn't finish watching the porno in the hotel room. Outside, beyond the thick gray vinyl curtains insulating us from the outside world that we had pulled across the window for privacy it was cold and windy, the days becoming shorter. Soon it would be winter and we'd be counting the months until we went back to our cocooned Jewish Socialist camp—the place where we slept inside see-through mosquito netting and would never need thick curtains to protect us.

Later, once we had stopped watching, Mark took a video camera out of his backpack. We didn't know he had brought one. Now that we had watched a porno, he told us, we were going to make our own. He moved around the room pretending to film us, telling us to move our legs this way, raise our arms that way, though we had been fully clothed all evening. We laughed at him then, and he laughed too, and then we decided we should go down the hall to swim in the hotel pool. Lynn and I changed into our bathing suits in the bathroom. After playing in the water, splashing and shoving each other, doing somersaults and handstands with our heads near the bottom of the pool so straight our feet stuck out perfectly like upside down ducks cooling off their bodies in a pond, we came back to the hotel room and collapsed, too young to begin thinking yet about all of the things that wouldn't last forever. Despite our best intentions to force it, the adult world had not quite yet descended on us. We slept like babies, the four of us in the same bed for the rest of the night.

My Russia Ukraine

My family loves communing with our deceased relatives on cemetery visits. This has always felt creepy for my brother Ed and me.

"It just freaks me out," Ed, who is named for our dad's father, whispered to me in Toledo back in the 1980s when we were kids, "looking at my full name on a gravestone." We trailed behind our mom and dad, sulking. Once we got to the grave, our parents told my brother to stand next to his dead grandfather and smile so they could take a picture.

It was strange, it's true, but I understand why they did it. It was their way of remembering their family and their history. Our grandfather, Ed, our *Zadie,* as we would have called him had he lived longer, died in 1949, when our dad was seven. He was sent on a ship to the Admiralty Islands in the Pacific Ocean in 1944 during World War Two, returned with pancreatic cancer, and died a couple years later.

My parents tried to teach me my Eastern European history, but Zionism got in the way. Rather than being interested in most of my family being from Russia and Ukraine (they called it "Russia Ukraine"), I was much more fascinated in what was happening to the east of Europe, in Israel. Friends used to tease me that I knew far more about Israeli history—the make-believe version—than the histories of Europe and the U.S.

In the last several weeks, however, I've been re-reading a history of my father's side of the family, the stories of many who are buried in the Jewish cemeteries we used to visit. My father's aunt, my great-aunt Esther, wrote it before she died of cancer in 1993, when I was 23. My father convinced her to write what she remembered, once she became ill. Great-aunt Esther was short and feisty. She smoked cigarettes in her bathroom with the door closed and the vent on high and always chewed mint gum. She wore black and white checkered suits and bright red lipstick. At her funeral in 1993 the undertaker put light pink lipstick on her. "It doesn't look anything like her," my mother said to me as we stood together looking at her in the casket. "Aunt Esther never wore pink."

"It is upon their gentle urging that I write a history of our ancestors," she wrote at the beginning of her 35-page account, in flowing cursive in a spiral notebook, full of scratch marks and crossed out words, "so that they may have knowledge of their roots." A yellowed photocopy has been sitting in the bottom of a box of mine for decades. I was 23 when she died in 1993 and I remember skimming through the pages, but admittedly, I wasn't all that interested. I had recently moved to Israel to attend graduate school in Jerusalem and to get away from my family.

I grew up in Chicago and in the summers we drove to Toledo and Detroit to visit our relatives. It was usually on Sundays when we were leaving town, just before getting on the highway heading back, that we'd stop at the Jewish cemeteries to say hello to our dead family members.

I was dreaming of things far beyond midwestern graveyards, like working in a field picking tomatoes on a kibbutz in Israel, tilling the land and putting down roots, starting a new life with other young Jews who, like me, had cut the branches from their families in the U.S. and left their old lives behind. Of course Israel's history, which I believed to be true at the time, was a fabricated past, solidified as a brand. I had sentimentalized this Jewish homeland, was blinded from the legacy of its myth that ignored Palestinian history. I turned away from my family's history, too, in exchange for the fantasy I believed would ground me, the dream I was taught that said Israel was "a land without a people for a people without a land."

At the cemetery in Detroit, after taking Ed's picture next to our grandfather's grave, my parents told me to say hello to Rose's grave, my great-grandmother for whom I was named. She came to the U.S. from Belarus and died in 1955. On the car ride back to Chicago, my dad reminded me, again, as he had done many times before, that I was named for Rose, his grandmother.

Even as a freshman in college I was still annoyed with these Midwest graveyard visits. When we went to the Toledo Jewish cemetery in 1988 I was feigning a rebellious streak while my love for Zionism and Judaism—words that were synonymous to me at the time—was growing. The previous summer I had gone on my first trip to Israel, an eight-week summer high school program in Hod Hasharon, just outside Tel-Aviv. I had seen tons of Israelis with tattoos and had heard the Jewish lore that said Jews who had tattoos couldn't be buried in a Jewish cemetery. But once I saw secular Israelis—who also hung out at the beaches on the High Holidays which seemed of the new world to me, a contrast to the long days I spent in synagogue in the old world diaspora—I decided I wanted one too. My middle name is Rose so I chose a small, dime-sized rose tattoo near my hip. I didn't want a stem despite the tattoo artist's suggestion to add some green color to the red flower. As a result, the rose has always looked suspended, groundless. It didn't take the artist more than a few minutes to make it. Seemingly permanent, the needle goes no more than two millimeters under the skin. It's also quite faded now.

When I got it in 1988, a year after my first trip to Israel, I wasn't thinking of my great-grandmother, Rose, for whom I was named, but of my middle name. Even more than this, though, I was thinking of my Hebrew name, Shoshanna, which also means Rose, and which I believed connected me more deeply to the land and language of the Israel I was already in love with.

At the Toledo cemetery that day in 1988 I swaggered up to one of the caretakers, my hand on my hip, touching my tattoo through my jeans as though it tethered me to something larger, perhaps blasphemous, despite it not having a rooted stem. I told the caretaker I had recently gotten a tattoo.

"What Jew will bury me, huh?" I asked, scoffing at the man. My father overheard me and rolled his eyes.

But the caretaker called my bluff. He wasn't rattled by an annoying teen trying to get a rise out of an older Jew.

"I'll bury you, honey," he quipped, stopping me in my bravado tracks, "Just let me know when it's your time."

Looking back now I think my decision to get that small rose tattoo, while seemingly couched in rebellion was also, in my warped thinking, an opportunity to align myself with Israel's secular society. In Israel, I could feel proud as a Jew walking around with a tattoo and going to the beaches on the High Holidays. Now, however, I wonder if it was an unconscious desire to remain connected to my great-grandmother Rose, after all, and to all of my family's European history, those that came from, and escaped from, Russia Ukraine.

I wasn't as much of a rebel as I thought. I was simply in between worlds, on the threshold between childhood and adulthood while also longing for an Israel I thought I knew, not caring about my roots in Europe, or about Palestinians who had long been living in Palestine and those who were forced to flee. I believed, as I had been taught, that the land we called Israel had been a land without people. Dreaming of Israel's mere existence made me happy. Who wouldn't be, my magical thinking told me, walking on stones thousands of years old where "my" ancestors had lived?

The fantasy I had developed about Israel served two purposes. First, believing in the Zionist dream, the nationalistic notion that Israel was righteous and just, worth defending and fighting for, satisfied my political inclinations: this delusion filled some emotional need I had to feel selfless about large causes. Second, daydreaming about it gave me meaning and purpose, a feeling of superiority over the mundane everyday existence of teenage angst in the U.S. "If I could just get back to Israel," my Jewish teenage friends and I said to each other, depressed and anxious, once we had returned from the eight-week trip we attended when we were 16, "everything will be okay." We didn't talk much about what exactly would be "okay," or why we felt this way, or even what we would actually do once we arrived in Israel, how we'd make a living, grow a career, pay taxes. Our world, though we believed we were left-wing, didn't have a wide enough range for us to consider the indigenous Palestinians who had been living in Palestine, were from there, and had been displaced, ethnically cleansed, held under military occupation so that liberal Zionists like us could develop our love for the land without ever feeling bad about it. Besides, we were mostly upper-middle class Zionist Jews whose parents had paid for our trips to Israel. We just cared about getting back there; it was a fantasy, an unrealized ideal love. We'd figure out the rest.

If we didn't get back there, we'd be okay, too. We were in the U.S. Like a love affair that takes place outside the mundanity of one's everyday life, staying just enough out of reach to pine for it, so too, was Israel outside of us enough to intoxicate us and make us long for it. If an ideal state is never realized, it remains unrequited.

Removing oneself from Zionism, as from any ideology, can be difficult. The political and the personal—the two essential elements that make Zionism work—are deeply intertwined. Its ethos taps into the hearts of young Jews and makes them feel like they are living for something big, far beyond themselves. To separate the political and the personal, the Zionist must recognize first, that Israel is a colonial machine, that its goal is to take all of Palestine while getting rid of Palestinians, to colonize the land while pretending to have always been there—to make new stones Zionists walk on indistinguishable from the ones that were always there. The Zionist will need to admit that believing in Israel's mythos serves not only an ideological and nationalistic purpose, but that it also fills this deeply personal, emotional need as well.

This duality, this nostalgic colonialism, seeps into the Zionist making it hard to untangle, despite the facts, stories, and true history the Zionist might be told. Undoing Zionism requires an uprooting, a deeply unsettling paradigm shift that what was previously believed was a myth. But one of the rarely acknowledged harms of myths is that it's not merely that they are untrue, it's that they are all-consuming, blotting out other narratives, other possibilities, and other aspects of our own identity.

Disinterest in my family's Eastern European roots also manifested when it came to food. My Baubi made beet borscht, brisket, tzimmes, rugelach, and homemade gefilte fish, and tried, and failed mostly, to teach me how to make these too. Though my sweet tooth loved her chocolate rugelach. I remember as a girl watching her put all her strength into pushing the rolling pin over the dough to make it thin enough to roll as I sat at her kitchen table watching her, mesmerized by the strength in her arms.

When I moved to Israel in the 1990s I learned to make foods closer to my heart like hummus (I had been taught it was the national food of Israel) and baba ganoush and falafel. The Jews I knew in the U.S. used a blender to make hummus; in Israel I crushed the chickpeas and garlic by hand.

My thinking had become dichotomous. My Israeli "history" matters, my Eastern European history doesn't. For some reason my parents didn't carry this tension, perhaps because they were older, chronologically closer to their European roots than I was, closer to the Holocaust than I was. Room existed for them to be Zionists while also caring about their European history. They supported my love of Israel and were confused and hurt when I undid my Zionism. Another problem for the Jew who separates from Zionism is that your family won't understand you, may not like you, perhaps may hate you. They might think you don't care about history even though you do, even if you may feel untethered.

As I've been re-reading my great-aunt Esther's history of our family, I haven't been able to put it down. My paternal great-grandfather, Benjamin Shulman, was born in "Russia Ukraine" in 1880. He was conscripted into the Russian army in 1901, and came to the U.S. in 1905, before the 1918 pogroms in Ukraine.

"My Dad left Russia Ukraine in 1905, came by steerage to Ellis Island on the Hamburg Line," my great-aunt Esther wrote. I noticed she had crossed something out where she wrote that her dad had "left" Russia. When I looked closer, I saw that she had originally written, "escaped from," instead of "left." The original sentence actually reads, "My Dad ~~escaped from~~ left Russia in 1905, came by steerage on the Hamburg Line." To *leave* rather than to *escape*. I don't know why great-aunt Esther changed her sentence but she must have wanted to believe her parents had some sort of agency over their choice to leave their "Russia Ukraine," so that they didn't sound helpless or weak.

When I was a young Zionist, I heard the stories of Palestinians who, *if* they had been in Palestine—even this assertion, "if," was questionable to us young Zionists as we had been taught the desert was empty—had chosen to leave. Of course, this was an effort to sanitize the Palestinian expulsions and ethnic cleansing that occurred when Israel became a state and which still occurs today.

I just read in great-aunt Esther's notes that a great-great uncle of mine was a dressmaker in Odessa. He had a small shop "down near the Black Sea of Russia Ukraine." Great-aunt Esther's mother (my great grandmother Rose) told her granddaughter that "when she was sixteen she worked for her uncle, sewing for hours by candlelight near the Black Sea."

I longed for the Mediterranean Sea, not the Black Sea. Instead of tracing my family back three generations, I could, as a Zionist, draw a line from me to thousands of years earlier in Zion, my homeland. "Your soul is here," the posters at the youth aliyah desk in Chicago boasted, "Bring your body over." On one poster a woman sits alone on a beach, content, reflecting. She wears a simple one-piece black bathing suit and a big beige sun hat looking out calmly at the teal blue Mediterranean Sea.

It was easy to believe a mythical place was my home because messages all around me told me so. The synagogues my family attended were Zionist. At Hebrew school we drew maps of Israel and sang songs longing for the land. When we learned about European history, it was only within the context of the Holocaust, not even about when masses of Jews left Russia Ukraine in the early 20th century, never as a celebration of Jewish European life. One of my few memories of learning anything about Europe was when I was 10 years old and my Hebrew teacher made us sit still and be quiet for five minutes. "So we could feel what Anne Frank felt when she was hiding in the annex," she told us.

At the overnight Jewish summer camp I attended we created maps of Israel with ice cream, licking our fingers and flirting with each other as the ice cream melted in our hands, Jerusalem, Tel-Aviv, and Haifa literally beneath us at our fingertips. But, we didn't mention Bethlehem, Ramallah, or Nablus. The word Palestine never came up, for it did not exist in our hearts or in the histories we read that took place after 1948. We Israeli-danced outside on the basketball court, fantasizing about moving to our homeland. When I arrived in Israel at age 16 for the eight-week summer program and set foot on the land, finally, for the first time, I felt I had consummated the unrequited wandering of the diaspora. Everything before that trip was Zionist foreplay, like visiting dead European relatives I didn't care about and would no longer have to say hello to in midwestern cemeteries. The anticipation built for years, going was the ultimate fulfillment. My soul was there, as the posters showed me. I had brought my body over. Like the woman in the poster, I too, could sit alone on the beach in a simple one-piece black bathing suit and a big beige sun hat, looking out calmly at the teal blue Mediterranean Sea.

Ironically as someone who had been trying to ignore her European roots, I always marveled on all my trips to Israel at how "European" it felt. This was the plan, of course, the branding, to create a white, European colonial political project in the middle of the Middle East, one where someone like me could shed her old world Jewish European roots in a very European kind of way.

When I walked the streets at age 16 for the first time in marvelous wonder at the beauty of Israel and the even more magnificent Jerusalem, I told myself I was home. On subsequent trips when I returned so many times to walk on Jerusalem's limestone to see the light hitting the rock in late afternoon turning it pink and gold, the smells of sumac and cumin wafting through the alleyways of the shuk, I told myself I was home. But those things weren't my home. The land is Palestine. Of course, these nostalgic colonial fantasies the

Zionist has, both personally and politically, blinds the Zionist from seeing accurately.

Above all else, Zionism has been a catastrophe for Palestinians. It has resulted in generational trauma, expulsion, and displacement. And Zionism has been harmful to Jews because it has destroyed their ability for empathy and compassion. Like racism and colonialism—for Zionism is these things—it damages both victim and perpetrator.

Of course Israel does not want to solve the problems it has created and is determined to continue building the brand so that young Zionists will keep falling in love with its myth. "A civilization which justifies colonization—and therefore force—is already a sick civilization, a civilization which is morally diseased," Césaire asserts in *Discourse on Colonialism*. For Zionists who truly separate from Zionism they will become horrified when they see the moral disease that has been done in their name, in the place they were taught by people they trusted the most who told them it was okay to call that place home.

I wonder if my great-grandfather Benjamin mourned when he "escaped from" his home, his Russia Ukraine. I just read that he was from Katrinislav, a city in South-central Ukraine. Katrinislav was renamed Dnipropetrovsk in 1926, and then shortened to Dnipro in 2013. He married my great-grandmother, Rose, just before they left Russia Ukraine.

It's unfortunate that my childhood Zionism taught me to be prone to nostalgia, to sentimentalize the past, both politically and personally. Some might call this the human condition, perpetually pining for things out of one's reach, making sure something we think we love remains in an ideal state. For me this was Zionism. It may seemingly look like love but like a wolf in sheep's clothing, Zionism is an ideology that inflicts an enormous amount of pain and suffering onto others. The nostalgia I felt for Israel growing up was cultivated by a very seductive propaganda campaign, bound up with a more concerted political ideology designed to obscure a colonial, violent past.

Even now that I've separated from Zionism, I'm still prone to nostalgia. It's creeped up on me again today while reading my great aunt-Esther's history of her father, my great-grandfather's "Russia Ukraine."

Perhaps if I had been more interested in the real place my family was from, rather than the manufactured brainwashing I believed about Israel, I might have visited Russia Ukraine and returned to the midwestern graves to tell my relatives who are buried there about it.

A friend of mine who is also no longer a Zionist recently told me that he had visited Russia and Ukraine in the 1990s. He said even though he was, like me, in love with Israel at the time, he remembers even now, decades later, what it felt like to take the train down the length of Ukraine. "It was such a different feeling from Israel," he told me, "to feel, really feel, that my family actually came from there, that my roots were really there. I never felt that in Israel."

I wonder if my great-grandfather longed for the views of the Black Sea, the quarries and the bedrock, the mountains, the fields, the poplar and birch trees, the woods, the river that runs through Dnipro. Perhaps before he "escaped," before he "~~left,~~" he marveled at the beauty of his home, too, as he walked the streets of his "Russia Ukraine."

"He told me of the times he didn't have enough warm clothes or shoes for the rough winter snows, as he ran the errands for his mother," my great-aunt Esther wrote in her notebook about her father. "But I remember how he often spoke of how sweet and delicious was a ripe apple off a Russia Ukraine tree."

Then again, maybe my great-grandfather wasn't prone to nostalgia like I am, and didn't have time to long for his own country, to ponder rootlessness and sentimentality, to be a rebellious teen with a stemless rose tattoo. Instead, my great-grandfather grabbed the apple from a very rooted tree, I am sure, as he walked the streets of his Russia Ukraine, preparing to escape so that his daughter Esther might one day from the U.S. write that he had only left.

—Liz Rose Shulman—

The Nazis Are Coming

When the 11 Nazis unfolded their banner that screamed, "Holocaust—Six Million Lies," they were hit with eggs and rocks by the 2,500 counter-demonstrators who came to protest. A police helicopter hummed and lingered over the crowd. After seven minutes, the Nazis retreated, hiding under their swastika-painted shields. It was Sunday, October 19, 1980 and the Nazis had obtained a permit to march—exercising their right to free speech—at Lovelace Park in Evanston, Illinois, the suburb just north of Chicago and home to Northwestern University. The counter-demonstration was sponsored by the B'nai B'rith Hillel Foundation of Northwestern and other Jewish and local interfaith groups in Evanston. The Nazis had originally applied for the permit to hold their rally a month earlier on Yom Kippur, Saturday, September 20. The mayor at the time, James Lytle, turned them down for that particular day but granted them the permit for October 19.

I was 10 years old in 1980, and I remember the day of the march. It was four miles from my home. I had just returned from Sunday school at our synagogue in Skokie, the suburb just west of Evanston. Oddly, no one mentioned the march, or perhaps, I just don't remember anyone talking about it. That day my Sunday school teacher, an old Israeli woman with long droopy eyelids smothered with thick bright green eyeshadow, had us paint the State of Israel with our fingers on heavy construction paper. After sketching the outline of the tiny country, we dipped our fingers into plastic bowls of green, yellow, blue, and red paint and made a mess on our paper as we tried, and failed, to color within the lines of the country's borders.

With our moist, dirty fingers, we created grass and mountains and water and flowers in an abstract place that felt far away from us. It was sexual, of course, to be fingering a country that we were slowly being taught to love, but we were prepubescent children, unaware of the eroticization of things like land—and the landscape of our own bodies—that would be instilled in us as we got older. I didn't realize at the time, but later, my relationship with Israel would become akin to a lover to me. When we finished our finger painting we lined up the papers by the window sill and compared. But the real one, a cold official map of Israel twenty times larger than our individual 8x11s, loomed, staring at us from across the room. Pitted against the authentic State, every student's Israel looked misshapen, distorted, colored out of the lines, dripping like it was melting.

When I came home from Sunday school, I prepared for the Nazi march. I ate Cheetos at the kitchen table and then walked downstairs and hid in the basement of our house in a corner under the ping pong table. Though I had heard that the Nazis were marching, I'm not sure where I knew this fact from, since my memories of it seem to consist of me feeling alone. I was scared. I bit my nails until they bled, thinking of Nazis in brown uniforms with shiny black belts and my melting State of Israel, too, from earlier in the day, as I heard my family above walking in the kitchen. After a few minutes I got bored and my fingers were sore, but I wasn't moving. The Nazis were coming. A bit of green paint had remained on my hand. It mixed with some orange Cheetos crumbs. On my palm, I drew an imagined distance from Jerusalem to Tel-Aviv with my finger. After hiding for about an hour my father came downstairs and saw me in a fetal position under the ping pong table.

"What are you doing?" he asked.

"I'm hiding from the Nazis," I answered.

"Get upstairs," he quipped, "and finish your chores."

I had learned about the Holocaust for the first time a few years earlier at Hebrew school at the same synagogue from the same old Israeli woman with the glinting green eye shadow. I remember one day in particular when she wanted us to feel what it was like to be Anne Frank hiding in the attic. That day, she made our class sit quietly for five minutes. She used a kitchen timer and told us we needed "to know what it felt like to have to be still all day like the Franks up in the attic." It didn't work. After a few minutes, one student said he had to pee and another farted and then everyone giggled. We were mostly upper middle-class ten-year-old Jews learning what it was like to be oppressed but we had treated the Anne Frank activity like a game and we just didn't get it.

Now, though, I wonder if learning about Anne Frank experientially that day made more of an impression on me than I thought for, like others, I've been obsessed with her story for as long as I can remember. I've read all the different versions of her diary several times (I return to Melissa Mueller's biography every few years). I've written bad poetry about Anne, for Anne, seen every play and film that I could. I've scoffed at the ways Anne's diary has been sanitized, too, captured by Cynthia Ozick in her 1994 essay, "Who Owns Anne Frank?" "The diary has been bowdlerized, distorted, transmuted, traduced, reduced," Ozick writes, "it has been infantilized, Americanized, homogenized, sentimentalized; falsified, kitschified."

My obsession with Anne Frank came from her darker moments, not the ones that have been universalized by readers into hopefulness, like the sentence Ozick calls Anne's most celebrated—and misused—slathered on Anne Frank posters and postcards worldwide that says, "I still believe, in spite of everything, that people are truly good at heart." Why is she remembered for this line, Ozick wonders, rather than the sentence she wrote three weeks before she was sent to Westerbork. "I see the world being slowly transformed into a wilderness," Anne writes, "I hear the approaching thunder that, one day, will destroy us too, I feel the suffering of millions." Ultimately, Anne's story doesn't end in the attic, where her diary stops. Her life ends like millions of others whose lives ended in the camps, Ozick writes:

Anne and Margot were dispatched to Bergen-Belsen. Margot was the first to succumb. A survivor recalled that she fell dead to the ground from the wooden slab on which she lay, eaten by lice, and that Anne, heartbroken and skeletal, naked under a bit of rag, died a day or two later.

Of course, I wasn't thinking about Anne's final days either when I hid under the ping pong table in 1980. I got a sense of Anne's increasing despair later when I read her diary again and then Mueller's biography and learned what happened once she got to Bergen-Belsen. Though I had nothing really to be scared of in 1980, I'm sure I must have been trying, in a childish candor, to relate to what happened to Anne, or at least to try to understand it. My obsession took hold then and never left.

Nathan Englander writes about a different kind of obsession with Anne Frank in his 2011 short story, "What We Talk About When We Talk About Anne Frank." The characters describe what they call the "Righteous Gentile Game," or the "Who Will Hide Me Game." It's just what they do, the character Deb says, when they talk about Anne Frank. "[I]n the event of an American Holocaust," she says, "we sometimes talk about which of our Christian friends would hide us." Ever since Englander's story came out, I've called this the Anne Frank Game, and I play it often though I'm not proud of it, most recently at an English Department meeting at the high school where I teach. I played the game by myself, while my Department Chair talked to us about Common Core standards and upcoming evaluations. Out of 37 English teachers—there are 40, but Jews are exempt, according to my rules—I came up with three colleagues I thought *might* hide me. I have no other rules, really, it seems, because I never get past the question of who would hide me. The "who" is the game. I suppose there should be more guidelines, such as do they get more points for hiding me longer than others, what kind of food would they bring me, would I have a toilet I could use, and, of course, what happens after the war. In my English Department, I was on the fence about one of the three; he'd say he would hide me, but his "yes" would be more about his need to appear politically correct. When it came down to it, I didn't actually think he'd take the risk of keeping me safe in his attic.

My looks also contributed to my obsession with Anne Frank I'm sure, for I was told often how much I resembled her. This happened a lot as a child, but when I was 22, a stranger, a woman from Belgium, said I looked just like Anne in the gift shop at the Anne Frank House in Amsterdam. It was 1992, and my father brought me to visit the house. Like millions of others before us I got the chills as we walked up the steep stairs behind the bookcase. But when I walked into Anne's room and saw the pictures of the movie stars on the walls—Ginger Rogers, Norma Shearer, the dancer Joyce van der Veen were just a few—I began to cry. Anne wrote about this in her diary:

> Thanks to Father, who had brought my whole collection of picture postcards and movie stars here beforehand, I have been able to treat the walls with a pot of glue and a brush and so turn the entire room into one big picture.

I looked at my father, then sure he would have done the same for me. It was when we exited the house onto Prinsengracht Street my that father gave me the map and told me to lead us. I had to learn to find my way, he said. He knew I was shook up, but for him, the best way to deal with my sadness was to teach me to move forward.

The Nazis that came to Evanston in 1980 were not the same Nazi group that applied for a permit to march in Skokie just three years earlier, on May 1, 1977. The leader of the National Socialist Party of America, Frank Collin, chose Skokie for that march because of the large number of Holocaust survivors—thought to be the biggest outside of Israel. According to the Illinois Holocaust Museum, in 1977 about 40,500 of the 70,000 residents of Skokie were Jewish, and around 7000 of these were Holocaust survivors. A long legal battle followed, resulting in a landmark free-speech decision in which the Nazi group, defended by the American Civil Liberties Union (ACLU), was granted the permit. Ultimately, however, Collin and his group decided not to march in Skokie and chose downtown Chicago instead. When we moved to Evanston in 1979 from Gainesville, Florida, people were still talking about it.

And for some reason I've never been able to understand, a couple years before I hid in the basement, my Hebrew teacher with the shimmering green eyeshadow had also told my class rumors that Adolf Hitler was alive and living in Africa.

"Why the hell would she tell you that?" my father asked later when I told him and my mother at dinner one night.

"Honey," my mother leaned into my father, "just let her talk."

I don't know why my teacher disclosed this. But I remember being almost as scared that day as I was in 1980. I did read later, claims that Hitler might have lived out his days in Colombia or Argentina, so perhaps my Hebrew teacher was referring to these rumors and got it wrong. I suppose the country where he might have lived doesn't matter, really, but if she—the adult in charge—was going to tell a bunch of eight-year-olds Hitler was alive, she could have gotten her facts straight.

Despite these fears I had when I was young, or perhaps because of them, I grew up with a strong Jewish identity. I was part of a large thriving Jewish community along Chicago's North Shore. I belonged to the progressive, Habonim summer camp whose ideals were rooted in Zionism. The Holocaust was over. In high school my Jewish friends and I wore stickers every year on Holocaust Remembrance Day that said, "Never Again," as we hugged each other tight. I'm sure at the time we believed the slogan to be true. We were strong and confident—we were not victims. We would never be like lambs to the slaughter.

As my Jewish identity deepened, so did my love for Israel. Of course, it began as a child, finger painting the tiny country—claiming and occupying the land in childlike terms—in Sunday school, but as a teenager it blossomed. In 1986, when I was 16, I got my first job at the local kosher butcher, Kosher City, in Skokie, to save money for my first trip to Israel. My parents said I needed to help pay for the eight-week program. The owner paid me $3.25 an hour, cash, under the table, and every Sunday for four hours I cut heads off fish and sliced cheese by the pound. My parents lovingly led me to believe that they couldn't have paid for the trip to Israel without the three hundred dollars I earned by myself.

Finger-painting an abstract version of Israel was like foreplay for me—arriving in Israel was the consummation. I fell in love and a few years later, in my 20s, I moved to Jerusalem to attend graduate school. Though I never made aliyah, I pretended I was Israeli when it was convenient for me to do so. I used the land as a playground. But my mystified love for the country was always different than daily life. My attempts to permeate the society were limited. I hadn't served in the army. My Hebrew was sufficient but not sophisticated. I didn't really like Israelis all that much; I just didn't seem to have that much in common with them. The year I lived in the graduate dorm Idelson, on the Mt. Scopus campus, most Israelis went home on the weekends—a reality vastly different from my college dorm experience in Madison, Wisconsin, a few years earlier, where everyone was drunk on the weekends. So I hung out with others who, like me, had come to Israel from somewhere else. I was no Sabra; I was the faux ex-pat on a student visa. A Diaspora Jew to the core. I played darts at Champs, the bar full of other faux ex-pats on Yoel Solomon Street near Zion Square. I had more in common with the Palestinian-American, Khalil, I met than Israelis in my graduate classes. Khalil and I dated for a year, and together, we used the country as the backdrop for our experimental 20s, drinking and smoking our way through the West Bank. And then there was Tavit, who I dated for two years. It seems that I had become more comfortable with the finger-painted blurry Israel I had created when I was 10 on the day of the Nazi march than the large real map across the classroom. I needed Israel misshapen and distorted, colored outside of the lines, I suppose; which is to say, I would long for it and define it in my own terms, but never fully penetrate it, and then return, and leave again.

But even the most official maps are blurry and distorted. I remembered that the large map in my Sunday school classroom, for example, highlighted the Jewish-Israeli cities, not Palestinian ones. The words Judea and Samaria spread across what I'd later learn was also called the West Bank. I'd gone to Ramallah and Bethlehem—two major Palestinian cities I didn't know anything about. Later, on subsequent trips when I'd return to Israel, I visited other Palestinian cities, too—Nablus, Nazareth, Jenin, Tulkarm. Checkpoints. Occupation. Apartheid.

Once I finished my master's degree in 1996, I got an apartment in Chicago and bought a shower curtain of a map of the world. There, in the Middle East, painted in pink, purple, and green was Lebanon, Jordan, Saudi Arabia, Syria. Israel was in the middle but there was no Palestine. I took my black sharpie and, after putting a slash mark next to Israel, wrote the word Palestine. It was a feeble step towards activism, one that only I and a handful of others who used my equally pitiable bathroom would ever see.

In the winter of 2010, when I was 40, I went back to Israel/Palestine again. This time, it was with 20 other Jews on a dual-narrative tour that exposed us to both the Israeli and Palestinian perspectives. We traveled together for 10 days.

One night, we stayed with Palestinian farmers who work for the Canaan Fair Trade olive oil factory in Jenin. I remember this last night drinking tea, eating, talking with our hosts. Late in the evening as the dusk was rolling into night I looked out the large window. From this particular view I didn't see the Occupation Wall. There were no soldiers. The voices of my hosts faded. It was silent. The hills and valleys went on as far as I could see. There were olive trees everywhere. It was green and plush. It was quiet and dark. I saw Arab-style homes built squarely into the landscape, lights dotting the hills. Inside the homes I couldn't see but pictured, families making dinner, kids doing their homework, a mother tucking her baby into bed. My mind rolled back to pre-1948. I saw—perhaps for the first time, really, finally, Palestine, the Palestine before it was taken. "More tea?" my host asked me as I turned away from the window.

Another night we stayed in Deheishe, the refugee camp established in 1949 just south of Bethlehem with Palestinian families who had agreed to host us. During dinner, we sat on large square pillows on the floor as our hosts served us warm pita and small plates of hummus, baba ganoush, tahini with parsley, za'atar with olive oil, chicken with rice. We smoked hookah afterwards and drank mint tea. The matriarch, Safa, said she doesn't try to leave Bethlehem anymore because she's never let through the checkpoints. Her children told us stories of Israeli soldiers kicking them, invading the refugee camp in the middle of the night. "Incursions," their mother said.

In my naïveté, Israeli soldiers had been objects of American Jewish girls' flirty behavior. To us they were hot. To Palestinians, they are the enforcers of the ongoing military occupation. I remembered this story when they stopped Khalil on our road trip to Eilat, the one when I was 16 on my first trip, when my friends dared me to make out with an Israeli soldier and ask him for his shirt. I approached one in the Russian Compound in Jerusalem outside a bar. The soldier had black curly hair and green eyes. As we made out he pushed me against the brick wall and I felt his M16 press against my thigh. "Is that your gun or are you just happy to see me?" I asked him, laughing and drunk. He gave me his shirt. In Deheishe, Safa's son told a story of watching an Israeli soldier point his M16 at his father's face. Then the soldier kicked his father in the shin until it bled. Her husband, Safa told us, was humiliated in front of his children. After hearing I was an English teacher, one of the daughters brought her English books out and showed me a passage she was reading. It was on the use of computer technology in the classroom. One of the pages had a map. The daughter pointed to Deheishe. "We live here," she said. Like my father did with me, I wanted to take her outside and empower her to find her way. But it was getting late, and besides, she already knew her way around the refugee camp like the back of her hand.

In the evening, as the dusk rolled into the camp, we went onto the roof and watched the rose and orange colors dance across the sky. We saw lights flicker above us from the neighboring hills—all Israeli settlements. Later that night, four of us women from the trip slept on the floor in a small, square room the father had built on top of their bedroom. We had thin individual mattresses and lots of blankets, but it was still cold. One woman read on her iPad. The other two slept.

I finally fell asleep, too, but I awoke in the middle of the night and was disoriented. I was thinking about the Israeli soldiers' incursions into the refugee camp the family had told us about that evening, but also making out with the Israeli soldier when I was 16. I began to feel sick. My mind spun back decades to when I hid from the Nazis in my basement when I was 10 after fingering my private distorted version of Israel. But I was 40 now and I felt ashamed for the jumps my brain was taking. I was in a Palestinian refugee camp staying with people who were forced here in 1949, and if things continue the way they are they'll never get to leave.

    I was up most of the night at Deheishe, and I bit my nails until they bled. At one point I played the Anne Frank game. I determined that only one of the three women who lay on the floor would hide me if there was another Holocaust—the one with the iPad. Outside it was quiet. The children in the house had been asleep for hours. Earlier, I had heard the sound of pots and pans in the kitchen, but the noise had long dissipated. When I was still I began to feel some warmth, but I felt alone. I looked at my palm then, and under the blanket where no one could see, I drew a line from Jerusalem to Tel-Aviv, thinking of all the places and things in between that I've missed.

ACKNOWLEDGMENTS

- Timothy Beal, *Religion and Its Monsters* (Routledge, 2002)
- Aimé Césaire, *Discourse on Colonialism* (Présence Africaine, 1955)
- Meghan Daum, *Selfish, Shallow, and Self-Absorbed: Sixteen Writers on the Decision Not to Have Kids* (Picador, 2015)
- Joan Didion, "Goodbye To All That." *Slouching Towards Bethlehem* (Farrar, Strauss and Giroux, 1961)
- George Eliot, *Daniel Deronda* (William Blackwood and Sons, 1871)
- Nathan Englander, "What We Talk About When We Talk About Anne Frank," (*The New Yorker*, 2011)
- Anne Frank, *The Diary of a Young Girl: The Definitive Edition* (Doubleday, 1995)
- Jack Halberstam, *Skin Shows: Gothic Horror and the Technology of Monsters* (Duke University Press, 1995)
- Dzongsar Jamyang Khyentse, *What Makes You Not a Buddhist* (Shambhala Publications, 2007)
- Yitzhak Laor, *The Myths of Liberal Zionism* (Verso, 2009)
- Amos Oz, *In the Land of Israel* (Am Oved Publishers, 1983)
- Amos Oz, *Under This Blazing Light* (Cambridge University Press, 1996)
- Cynthia Ozick, "Who Owns Anne Frank?" (*The New Yorker*, 1997)
- Ilan Pappe, *The Ethnic Cleansing of Palestine* (Oneworld Publications, 2006)
- Motti Regev and Edwin Seroussi, *Popular Music & National Culture in Israel* (University of California Press, 2004)
- Sara Libby Robinson, *Blood Will Tell: Vampire as Political Metaphors Before World War I* (Academic Studies Press, 2011)
- Freddie Rokem, "Postcard From the Peace Process" (*Palestine-Israel Journal*, 1955)
- Edward Said, "Zionism From the Standpoint of its Victims" *The Question of Palestine* (Vintage Books, 1979)
- Rose Surnow, "I Gave a Handy at Jew Camp" (*Vice*, 2012)

Notes on Previous Publications

Thanks to the editors of the following journals in which essays from this book originally appeared in some form:

Angel City Review. "'Rose-Red City Half as Old as Time.'"

Litbreak. "A Meandering, Sometimes Agonizing Path."

Mondoweiss. "Once I Was Lit by Moonbeams"; "It's Their Birthright"; "Rereading Amos Oz a Year After His Death"; How Many More Orgasms Will be Had for Zionism?"; "O Jerusalem—Please Forget Me."

Punctuate. "While He Was Stopped by Soldiers."

Tablet. "Was Dracula Jewish?"; "The Stamp Collector": "My Jerusalem Love Affair"; "Holy Land Harps"; "First Porno"; "The Nazis Are Coming."

THANKS

I am incredibly grateful to Emily Perkovich for publishing this book. And huge thanks to the editors, writers, and friends—some who became a part of this book, and others who helped me become a better writer and thinker about Zionism and Judaism, about Israel and Palestine: Peter Beinart, Rich Blue, Michael Davis, Haidar Eid, Danny Friedlander, Elisheva Gordon, Phil Hammack, Adam Horowitz, Husam Jubran, Aryeh Katz, Garnett Kilberg-Cohen, Cynthia Kling, Danny Kuttab, Hovsep Nalbandian, Miriam Nauri, Abby Nimberg, Jonathan Ofir, Meghan O'Gieblyn, Nancy O'Rourke, Ilan Pappe, Paul Rivlin, Brant Rosen, Khalil Sahour, Eric Saranovitz, Michael Trigilio, Tony Trigilio, Purag Der Vartanian, Phil Weiss, and Manal Yazbak Abu Ahmad. And the biggest thanks to my parents, Claire and Stan Shulman, for giving me room to figure out who I am, and for loving me in the process.

www.ingramcontent.com/pod-product-compliance
Ingram Content Group UK Ltd.
Pitfield, Milton Keynes, MK11 3LW, UK
UKHW031311030225
4420UKWH00050B/1053